CREATIVE
HOMEOWNER®

Porches and Sunrooms

PLANNING AND REMODELING IDEAS

Roger German

CREATIVE HOMEOWNER®, Upper Saddle River, New Jersey

CREATIVE
HOMEOWNER®

A Division of Federal Marketing Corp.
Upper Saddle River, NJ

Produced by WordWorks
Editor: Roger Holmes
Copyeditor: Sarah Disbrow
Proofreader: Evan Lambert
Indexer: Schroeder Indexing Services

Design and layout: Deborah Fillion
Illustrations: Mario Ferro
Cover design: Glee Barre

Creative Homeowner
VP/Publisher: Brian Toolan
VP/ Editorial Director: Timothy O. Bakke
Production Manager: Kimberly H. Vivas
Art Director: David Geer
Managing Editor: Fran J. Donegan

Manufactured in the United States of America

Current Printing (last digit)
10 9 8 7 6 5 4 3

Porches and Sunrooms: Planning and Remodeling Ideas, First Edition
Library of Congress Control Number: 2005922984
ISBN-10: 1-58011-268-4
ISBN-13: 978-1-58011-268-0

CREATIVE HOMEOWNER®
A Division of Federal Marketing Corp.
24 Park Way, Upper Saddle River, NJ 07458
www.creativehomeowner.com

Acknowledgments

I want to thank the folks at Creative Homeowner for the opportunity to write about porches and sunrooms, those wonderful spaces connecting the home to the great outdoors. I enjoy creating sentences, paragraphs, and chapters as much as I enjoy the hands-on work of fitting boards to beams to rafters to ceilings, and Creative Homeowner made this project a reality.

To everyone who worked on this book, Roger Holmes and Sarah Disbrow at WordWorks, art director Deborah Fillion at Image & Word, and illustrator Mario Ferro, many thanks for all your help. Photographers Jessie Walker and Donna Chiarelli, and especially Roger Bruhn and Rick Mastelli, who filled in on short notice, all provided photos that enhance and enrich the book.

I would also like to thank Bruce and Cheryl Hostetler at Hostetler Patio Enclosures in Milford, Nebraska; Ed Sarcia at Colebrook Conservatories in Winsted, Connecticut; and Mark Barocco at Renaissance Conservatories in Leola, Pennsylvania, for their generosity in letting us use their photographs of the handsome sunrooms and conservatories they make.

I want to thank my wife, Suzi, for her patience while I once again burned the candle at both ends.

And lastly, but most importantly, I want to thank all you porch sitters out there who like to linger with a good friend over a second cup of coffee or a late-evening glass of Cabernet Sauvignon in a special place that's neither inside nor out.

Contents

Introduction

I was re-introduced to porch-sitting by a good friend, a hot cup of tea, some over-stuffed chairs, and a swing. In the evening, there were candles, and when the weather was brisk, a blanket or two. Front porches say "Hello, how are you? Come on in and sit a spell." Porches, and their cousins sunrooms and conservatories, are about invitations, about welcoming friends and family, along with a bit of the outdoors, into your home.

Front porches soften the entrance to a home and smooth the transition from outside to in. Back porches or side porches can be equally inviting, offering a quiet place to shake out the kinks of travel, watch a thunderstorm approach, or read a book in the rain. Like porches, sunrooms and conservatories invite in the great out-doors, but they provide more shelter from inclement weather.

LOOKING BACK

Porches have been around since at least the ancient Greeks and Romans. In the United States they were all the rage in the first decades of the twentieth century but fell out of vogue in the 1930s and '40s. The demise of the front porch was reflected in several social and cultural changes and some material ones. Automobile traffic whizzing by precluded easy conversations with passersby. Then in the 1950s and '60s, air-conditioning rendered the cooling function of a large porch less important.

But the clincher was the introduction of indoor plumbing. Flush toilets meant a family could have a porch around back without the aroma of the backyard privy. Anybody who was anybody moved the porch to the side or behind the house to signal that, yes, we have indoor plumbing. The rise of the automobile also freed up the backyard from the need for a stable and the resultant fertilizer piles. In the transition years, front porches atrophied until they were merely a door with, perhaps, a pitched roof overhead to shield guests from the rain or, in some cases, no roof at all.

As families grew, a porch became a prime candidate for renovation into a room, or at least some breathing room. Some folks screened-in their porches to keep out bugs, and some went further and installed windows in the porch openings, giving birth to modern versions of the three-season room and the sunroom.

Three-season rooms and sunrooms have been around in one form or another probably since the time when glass was first used to block the wind but welcome in the sun. In nineteenth-century England, sunrooms with glass roofs, called conservatories, became popular among the industrial age's growing middle class. Previously restricted to homes of the aristocracy and the wealthy, conservatories provided comfort and social cache to a group acutely interested in acquiring both.

Whether driven by nostalgia for slower, less complicated times or by the opportunities for comfort and camaraderie a porch provides, porches are making a comeback. Old porches are being renovated, new ones added onto existing houses or designed as part of new houses.

Similar interest in three-season rooms, sunrooms, and conservatories has less to do with nostalgia than with the lifestyle amenities these rooms provide. Demand has spawned a large industry of custom builders and manufacturers that provide rooms for every budget and every style.

LOOKING AHEAD

Porches, three-season rooms, sunrooms, and conservatories resist hard definitions, but for the purposes of this book, there are differences worth noting.

Simply put, a porch is a covered entrance to a home, with enough room for a swing and a few easy chairs. Open to the air but protected from rain (unless it is blustery out, too), a porch may be supported by walls, wooden posts, or masonry piers. Older porches often rest on blocks or bricks set in the ground without consideration for the freeze-thaw cycle, which explains why the rooflines of many old porches resemble undulating sine waves.

Three-season rooms offer more protection from the elements by incorporating single-pane or vinyl windows and storm doors. A sunroom adds heating and cooling to the mix, with an insulated structure and, often, insulated window glass to keep utility costs within reason. Because the air is "conditioned," a sunroom is more a part of the house than a part of the outdoors; often an existing room can be modified into a sunroom by removing walls and adding glass in their place.

A conservatory is, in essence, a sunroom with a glass roof. With all that glass, conservatories resemble greenhouses both in their appearance and in the amount of heat that they absorb.

In this book we'll examine these rooms in some detail. We'll go over the pluses and minuses of each, including differences in construction and cost. We'll look at the possibilities of building from scratch, converting an existing space, and renovating or remodeling. We'll consider practicalities such as site orientation, heat gain and loss, heating and cooling options, codes, permits, materials, tools, and repair and maintenance. Along the way, there will be plenty of good ideas and pictures to inspire your own designs.

My hope is that this book will help you move from an initial, perhaps vague, desire to "do something" about adding or renovating a porch, sunroom, or conservatory to a completed project that suits your needs, your dreams, and your wallet. ■

CHAPTER 1

Design Possibilities

Adding or renovating a porch or sunroom can be a big project. To ensure rewards that match your efforts, careful planning is a must. Think of all the things you'd like to accomplish—more space for entertainment, an improved street facade, a quiet spot to enjoy some fresh air. These and other goals impose requirements on your project that must be expressed in wood, glass, concrete, and stone. This chapter will help you identify your needs and desires and introduce you to the process by which they can be translated into design ideas and then building plans.

THE PLANNING PROCESS

Many homeowners have a list of home improvement projects gathering dust in a drawer; things they really want to do but somehow can never get pulled together. To avoid having a project die on the list, the temptation can be strong to just jump in and get started while the idea and impetus are fresh. Scratch something out on a napkin and start pounding nails. There is some

If you're building a new house, you can incorporate a porch to take advantage of spectacular views as well as provide shade and sun at desired times of the day and the year.

This three-season porch renovation is attractive because someone took the time to design striking windows.

immediate gratification to this approach. But long term, it can be counterproductive, even expensively disastrous.

Make a Plan

When you're tackling a major project like adding or remodeling a porch or sunroom, it's always a good idea to take the time to produce a fairly detailed plan. Making a plan requires you to think of possibilities and practicalities, and to identify and solve potential problems. A good plan helps ensure that you get what you want at an affordable cost. The plan does not have to be the final

A porch addition can help transform a home. The extensive addition shown at top started out as the flat-roofed room shown above. With a lot of planning, the new roofline created an extra room.

Computer Design Programs

There are a variety of computer-aided design programs for homeowners who wish to design their own home or addition. They range in cost from free to several hundred dollars. All offer basic plan-drawing features; and some provide perspective features, even color 3-D renderings. The results look professional, but it may take a while to achieve them. As with most computer software, there is a steep learning curve on even the simplest programs. If you enjoy computer work, you can have fun with one of these programs. But you can produce an equally useful basic plan with a few sheets of graph paper and a pencil.

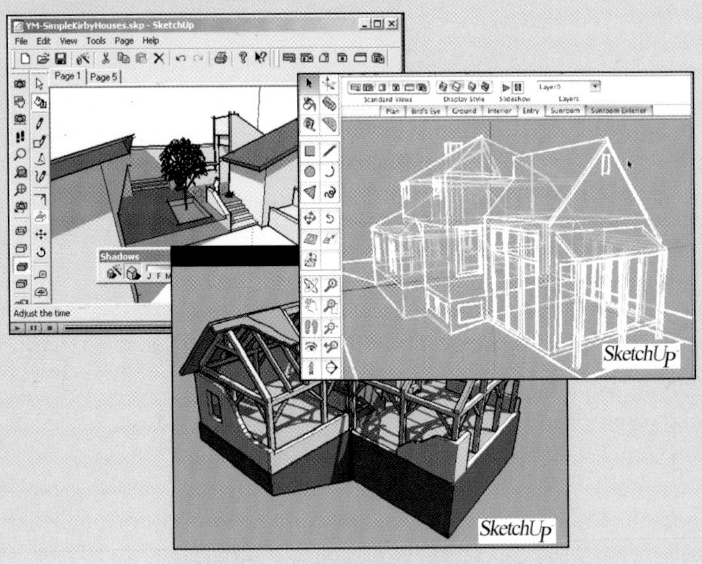

word. I've always considered remodeling projects as works in progress. But if you have a plan, it's easier to make alterations along the way and still be confident of reaching your destination.

Some homeowners are comfortable doing all the planning themselves; they enjoy the freedom to sketch, change, and doodle at leisure. If they have some drawing or drafting skill, they can even produce drawings detailed enough to obtain permits or guide construction. However, before deciding to be your own designer, remember that planning a project involves more than making good-looking drawings. Planning is a process of discovery that answers important questions: What do I want? How should it work? What should it look like? Can I afford it? This book will help you answer these questions.

Design Professionals

If you don't feel comfortable working out answers on your own, consider hiring a design professional to help you. An architect, design service, or designer-contractor has the experience and training to look at your project, refine and direct your ideas, or come up with new ideas for you. You can hire a design professional to help you produce ideas at the beginning of the planning process, or later to produce designs, or to manage the entire process from ideas through construction. (There are also computer programs that help homeowners design their own projects. See "Computer Design Programs," top left.)

Adding a porch to the west-facing side of this house provided a comfortable shaded area for late afternoon sitting and cut down heat gain in the living room behind the large ground-floor windows.

This conservatory adds a large room to this house, making it possible to enjoy a sunny brunch or relax under the stars.

WHAT DO YOU WANT?

Planning for any major home project is a little like planning a vacation. Before you pile in the car, you need to decide where you want to go. And before you decide where to go, you need to know what you want from your vacation. If you're after a romantic getaway, you'll probably rule out Disneyland. If it's a family vacation with your toddlers, Disneyland makes more sense than a three-day hike to a secluded lake. If money is tight but you just have to get away, a weekend at a modest but comfortable motel within driving distance may do the trick.

So, take time right at the beginning to think about what prompts your desire for a

How Big?

As you sketch possible plans, keep in mind several things about size. Like any living space, a porch or sunroom should be big enough to accommodate the activities you plan for it. It should also be in scale with the other elements of the house. Built too big or too small, a porch or sunroom can be both ugly and dysfunctional. That said, the cost of a porch or sunroom is only incrementally affected by adding a couple of feet of width or depth to it. As long as the addition isn't awkwardly out of scale with the existing house, a little bit too big is better than too small. I can't remember ever having a client complain that a porch we added was too large.

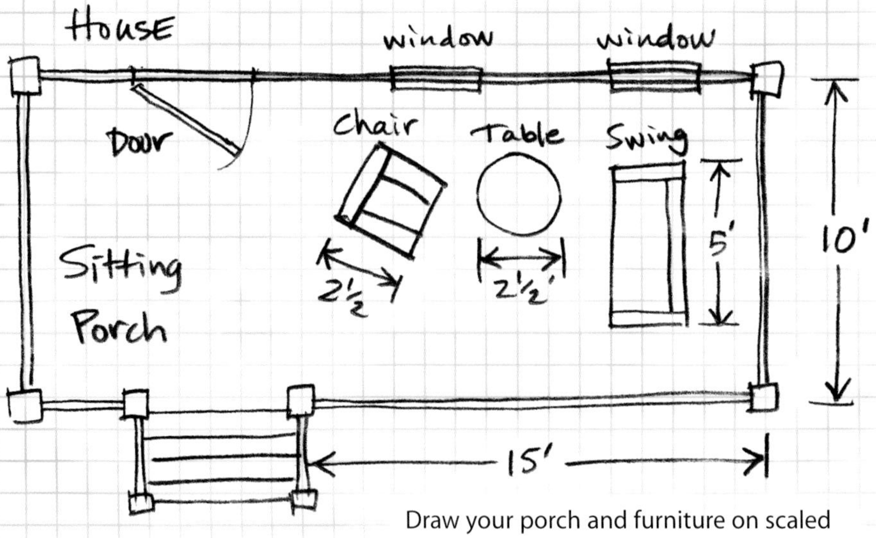

Draw your porch and furniture on scaled graph paper to make sure everything will fit.

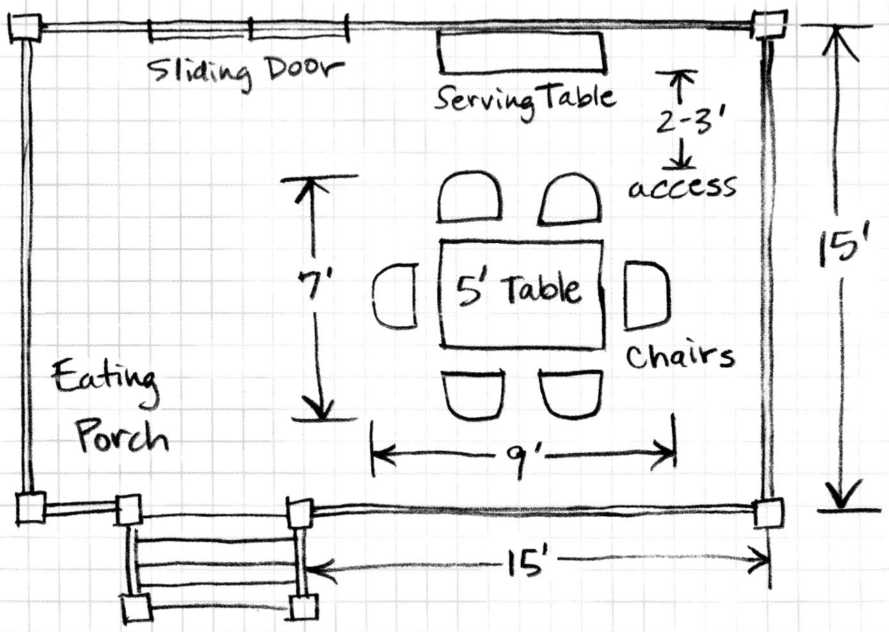

This porch provided an opportunity for some architectural playfulness. Its modest space is clothed in the grand style of a Greek temple. The mismatch in scale between the chairs and the structure adds to the charm.

porch or sunroom. Are you looking for a sunny spot, warm but not too hot, to read the paper on a Sunday morning? How about a quiet outdoor place on a summer evening to share a cup of coffee or a glass of wine with friends without getting eaten by mosquitoes? Perhaps you'd like an open-air room where you can keep an eye on your kids while they play. Or somewhere to entertain the overflow of guests when the extended family visits for the weekend. Do you want to be able to host an outdoor dinner when it's a bit too hot or too cold to sit on the patio? Perhaps you want to provide a more inviting entrance to your house. You'll probably find you have two or three desires at the same time.

Answers to questions about what you really want and need will help determine what you will build, where you'll build it, and how big it will be. Your answers will provide insight into the atmosphere you want to create with architectural style and furnishings.

They'll even help you plan for things that are often overlooked, such as how much and what kind of maintenance you're comfortable with.

Fresh Air and Sunshine

At their most basic, porches, sunrooms, and conservatories offer more fresh air or sunlight (or both) than are ordinarily available inside a house. An open-air porch provides an abundance of fresh air while protecting you to varying degrees from rain, wind, heat, cold, and direct sunlight. A three-season porch with screens or simple windows offers more protection against the elements in exchange for some restriction on fresh air and, sometimes, sunshine. A sunroom provides more sunlight and greater climate control than most three-season porches. A conservatory is a sunroom on steroids. It welcomes the sun as an open porch welcomes fresh air.

These characteristics can be altered and adjusted by the location of the structure with regard to the seasonal aspects of the sun and prevailing winds. Let's say you live in the northern latitudes and like the idea of the sun warming you as you read the morning paper on a new porch. To determine where to put the porch to accomplish your paper-reading desire, you'll need to consider the position of your house with regard to the path of the sun across the sky each day and over the course of the year. "Tracking the Sun," opposite, examines these

A porch offers a quiet place to read or keep an eye on the kids' play area, top.

This formal sunroom, left, is ideal for entertaining in all weather.

Tracking the Sun

To ensure that your porch or sunroom provides sunlight or shade when and where you want it, you need to plot the sun's daily and seasonal travels across your property. Over the course of a day, the sun rises in the east and sets in the west, and it is a simple matter to determine the sun's daily path across your property.

Over the course of a year, the sun also moves from south to north and back again, as shown at top right. (The earth is actually doing the moving, but the effect is the same.) In North America, the sun is farthest to the south on about December 21, the winter solstice. It is farthest north about June 21, the summer solstice. The angle at which sunlight falls on your property on these days depends on your latitude—how far north or south you live. The middle drawings show the difference.

The U.S. Naval Observatory offers a Web site that will calculate the position of the sun at various times of the year. (See "Resource Guide," page 212.) With this information, you can determine where and at what angle the sunlight will fall on possible porch or sunroom locations at any time of the year. You can also use this information to determine how you might configure roof and eave overhangs to control the amount of sunlight falling on the porch or sunroom, as shown in the bottom drawing.

Tracking the Sun

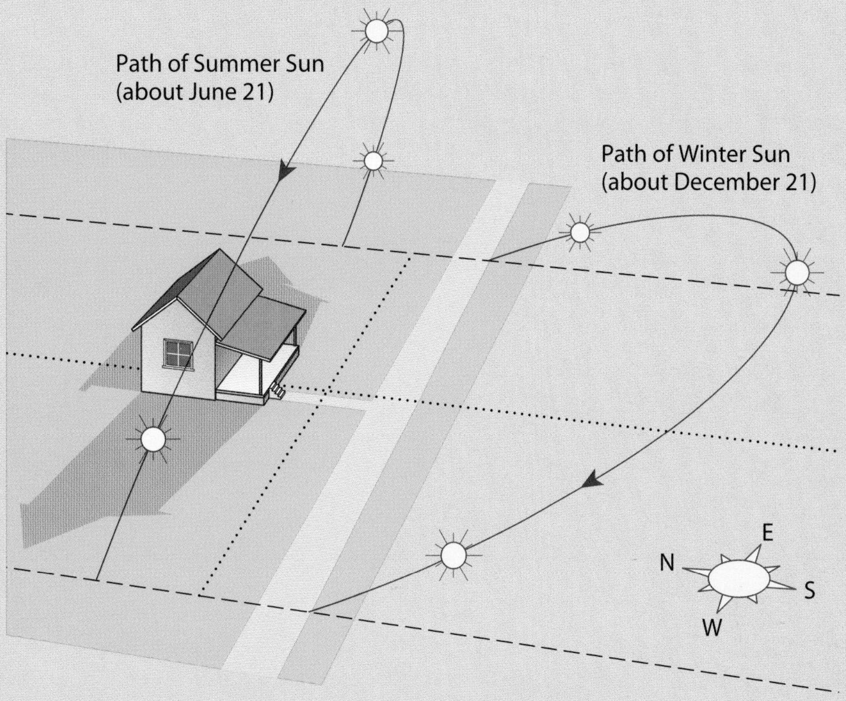

Sun Spots North and South

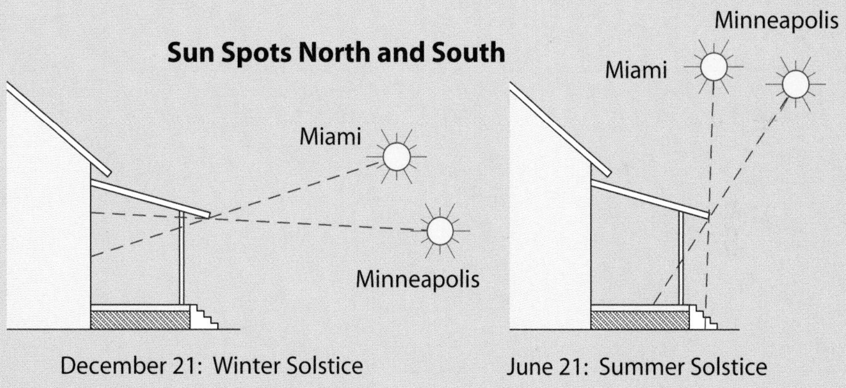

Blocking the Sun

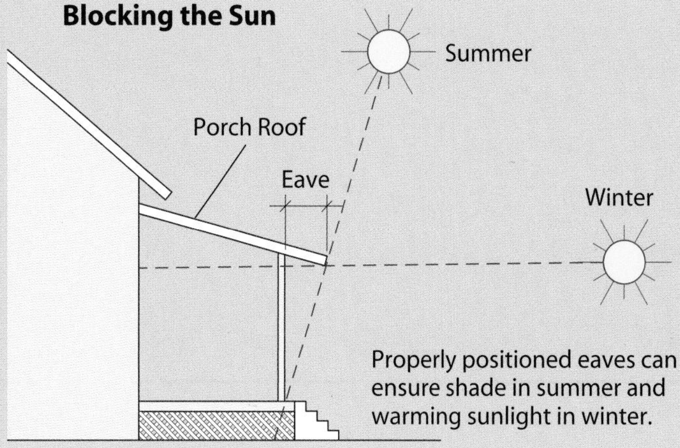

Properly positioned eaves can ensure shade in summer and warming sunlight in winter.

Orient a porch to catch the prevailing breezes of summer; then add screens to keep out bugs and to allow you to open doors into the house to circulate fresh air.

relationships further. If you have room for a porch with at least some eastern exposure, there's a good chance you'll be able to drink your morning coffee in the sun at least part of the year.

By gathering similar data about the prevailing winds in your area, you can position a porch to catch a breeze or, in areas like Nebraska, to avoid the stiffer, less pleasant winds that are prevalent for much of the year. If you've lived in the house for several years, you'll have a good idea of where the winds come from at different times of the year. If you're in a new house, check with neighbors or the local weather bureau.

Heat and Cold

Any structure that welcomes fresh air and sunshine is also going to be visited by heat and cold. Whether they are welcome, too, is a

SMART TIP

Sketches for Design. Before designing your porch or sunroom, make a sketch of your property. Identify the best views, direction of prevailing breezes, location of utilities and easements, and sources of nuisance noise or ugly views. These features, along with the path of the sun, may determine the addition's position and design.

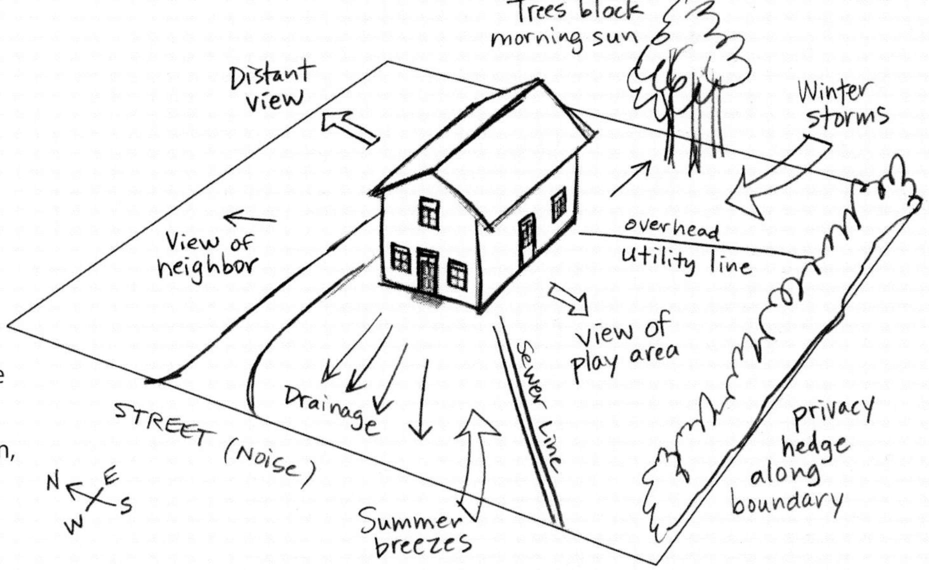

This well-thought-out addition combines an open-air porch, screened porch, and open deck, providing a multitude of possibilities for outdoor enjoyment.

matter of degree. The sun can work its radiant magic on a porch to keep you and your morning coffee warm. It can also make a sunroom into a mid-afternoon furnace. Sitting in a porch swing in a cool breeze and the shade of the porch roof can be just the ticket on a hot summer afternoon. But when the sun goes south in the fall, an open porch gets chilly fast.

So, when you're deciding what kind of structure will best suit your needs or when you're looking for a spot that best catches

An old-fashioned porch, left, offers a cool place to sit on a hot afternoon.

A well-positioned porch, below, welcomes early sun and is shaded in the heat of the day.

In chilly weather, the heat gained through these sunroom windows warms nearby sitters as well as adjacent rooms in the house.

Saving Energy

Energy consumption may not be a driving motivation for your project, but it should be a consideration. Properly planned, a porch, a three-season room, or a sunroom can help heat and cool the rest of your house. Improperly planned, they can cause discomfort and increase energy costs.

Open-air and screened-in porches temper the air to some degree before it enters your house. In summer a porch that shades the south side of a house can make a real difference in the afternoon temperature of an adjacent indoor room. Likewise, on a winter day a three-season porch can protect indoor rooms from biting winds and, if it has windows, even absorb enough heat to help keep adjacent indoor rooms cozy. Placed where they accumulate too much heat in the afternoon, these structures can make a neighboring indoor room uncomfortable in the summer.

A sunroom can be an effective aid to winter heating. As the sun moves south in the winter, sunlight penetrates farther into the sunroom, suffusing it with radiant heat. Floors and walls that incorporate concrete, brick, stone, or tile capture this free heat. These massive materials warm up slowly by day and slowly radiate stored-up heat in the evening. In moderate climates a sunroom may be usable year-round with no supplemental heat or cooling.

the sunlight and breezes, be sure to consider temperature. Here are some general rules of thumb: A porch or sunroom with an eastern or northern exposure will be warmed by the sun in the mornings. Later in the day, the house and the porch roof will block direct sunlight, so the space should be relatively pleasant in the afternoon and early evening, too. On the south or west side of your home, a porch or sunroom will be comfy in the morning but will cook in the afternoon and early evening sun.

An overhanging eave shades this shallow porch, top, from sun in summer and admits warming rays in winter.

A movable glass-and-screen window system takes full advantage of cooling summer breezes, left.

A ceiling fan can stir up some cooling air on a still day.

A Victorian-style porch defines the character of this house.

In my experience, the location of a porch or sunroom is usually a tradeoff. The best spot for sunshine may be adjacent to the bedroom, not the front entrance, where you'd rather have the porch. Or the splendid view is best seen from the coldest side of the house. You can only control the cold by changing the location or adding a heater. But there are a few ways to mitigate heat gain. On hot days when no breeze filters through the screens of a three-season porch or sunroom, a ceiling fan or two can move the air

Redecorating a porch or sunroom can effect large changes at less cost than rebuilding or remodeling.

around enough to give some relief. If heat gain is excessive, consider changing your plans from a three-season room to a sunroom that can be cooled by your central air-conditioning.

One of the best ways to control heat gain in any structure, from simple open porches to sunrooms, is by manipulating the position and extent of the roof's overhanging eaves. As the drawings on page 23 show, eaves can be placed to allow warming sunlight into a space in certain seasons or times of day, while shading the same space in other seasons or times of day.

This sunroom addition comfortably blends in with the house on both the outside, above, and inside, right.

COTTAGES

This plant lover's conservatory adds light and cuts heating costs.

REMODELING & CONVERSIONS

Many homeowners, particularly those with older houses, already have a porch. If it has been neglected, it may just need repairing. A porch, like any room in your house, can be redecorated, remodeled, expanded, or otherwise altered. A porch makeover may involve anything from a lick of paint and a new swing to complete rebuilding. You might change the look by sheathing square posts in classical columns made of fiberglass or by replacing the railings.

It doesn't take a lot of money to screen in an open-air porch, and it's not much more expensive to install glass for three-season use. Converting a porch to a sunroom is more difficult and expensive because of insulation needs. Instead, consider adding more windows to a suitable room in your house.

Deck Conversions

Decks are good candidates for conversion. A feature of suburban living almost everywhere, these open-air platforms are often hospitable only at certain times of the year. Fall and spring are usually pleasant enough on a deck, but summer can be brutally hot, and winter simply untenable. Converting a deck to a three-season porch or to a sunroom increases the number of days when you might be inclined to pass some time there. A three-season porch provides shade in the summer without compromising ventilation and fresh air. A sunroom can be a warm, sunny haven in winter. If you have room enough on your property, you can add a porch or sunroom to complement the deck. But if your spatial options are few, consider converting your deck.

Looking Good

Regardless of what you decide to build or where you decide to build it, you'll want your porch or sunroom to be an attractive addition to your house. Just about anything is possible. I've bent multilevel decks around curves, appended two-story curved-glass sunrooms, and enclosed a family-sized hot tub with a conservatory featuring steel columns and beams that supported a cedar-covered cathedral ceiling and window-wrapped cupola.

Built on an existing deck, right, this sunroom makes a harmonious addition to the house, below.

A simple corner porch protects the back door and adds interest to an otherwise uninteresting corner of the house.

The simplest structures are just boxes topped by shed, gable, or hip roofs. Just as often as not, they look as good as or better than elaborate and much more expensive structures. Why? Because a little extra thought and planning and a few well-chosen details can make even a rectangular box look as if it belongs with the rest of the house. Match the pitch of the shed roof on your porch addition to the pitch of your existing roof. If you can spend a bit more, match the Vermont slate shingles and copper gutters on the rest of your house. Or instead of using wooden 4×4 posts, support the porch roof with classical columns in the same style as the pilasters that flank your front door. If you're uncertain of your ability to integrate the new with the old, consult an architect or designer for help.

Enhancing the look of your home may be one of several major motivations for your

Situated to catch the afternoon sun in winter, this porch is a comfortable spot even when there's snow on the ground. In summer, the trees in the foreground will leaf out and provide afternoon shade.

SMART TIP

Practical Porches. When porches fell out of favor in the 1930s and '40s, new homeowners were often left in the rain while they fumbled for front-door keys. If you have a period house (or a new house for that matter) with an exposed front door, consider adding a porch as a functional way to dress up the entry.

Appending an eyebrow roof or a small shed roof to the wall above the door can keep the rain off but does little to enhance the look of your home. A tastefully designed porch can keep you dry as you enter and exit the house. It can also accommodate a couple of chairs or a swing. And it can add sparkle to a drab facade.

project. An attractive front porch can be just the detail your house needs to take it from livable but boring to a home with some real character. Providing a spot to sit and chat or read or sip coffee in the fresh air is a bonus. However, if you're contemplating adding a porch or sunroom to increase the value of your home, think twice. You'll probably spend more on the addition than you'll add to the home's resale value. These are projects better undertaken to enhance your life rather than fatten your pocketbook.

And that can be a liberating thought. If you're doing this for yourself, you don't have to guess what some prospective buyer might like. It doesn't really matter. Do what you like. A friend of mine added a porch onto the back of his house. Most people put sunrooms or decks in back and porches in front. He thought of that and played around with some ideas, but adding a deck at the back just did not look right. A porch gave him what he wanted, so that's what he built. And it looks as if it has always been there.

CONSERVATORIES

If you want to bask in as much sun as possible yet be protected from the elements, you should consider a conservatory. In its simplest form, a conservatory is a glass room, not unlike a greenhouse, with walls and roof of glass and as little structure as possible holding up the panes.

Sunrooms and some three-season porches can have a lot of glass in the walls. What sets a conservatory apart is its glass roof. Not just skylights, but an entire roof of glass. With glass around and above, a conservatory captures even more sunlight than a sunroom. It has all the advantages of a sunroom as well as providing a cozy spot for star gazing.

Conservatories also have all the disadvantages of sunrooms, and then some. Glass is a poor insulator; it provides little barrier to heat and cold. On a bright, zero-degree winter afternoon in Minot, North Dakota, a conservatory with fully insulated glass might warm up enough for you to sit in comfortably. But after sunset you'd need to find another spot. On a bright summer afternoon in Los Angeles, the same conservatory would be akin to a short-order griddle. Open the vents after sunset, however, and it might be a pleasant spot to dine under the stars.

Drapes give this sunroom, top, a distinctive style and, in the winter, additional insulation against the cold.

A bank of skylights transforms this porch, left, into a conservatory space along one side.

This welcoming conservatory, opposite, matches the style of the house perfectly.

Conservatory Challenges

Heating or cooling what is basically a glass room is one of several challenges that comes with a conservatory. You can build movable shades, or even buy built-in electric shades to close off the roof on hot days. You can install heated floor systems to keep the room hospitable on cold days. Or you can simply go with the seasons and use the room as the weather permits, basking in the warmth of a sunny midwinter afternoon or a pleasant summer day with scattered clouds blocking the sun's heat.

Building a leakproof glass roof is another challenge. Glass expands and contracts at a different rate from other construction materials, making a glass roof difficult to seal at the connections of glass to frame. In cold-winter climates, where the temperature inside a conservatory may fluctuate in a single day from freezing to 90 degrees, the difficulty of making water-tight seals is even greater.

Given these difficulties, many homeowners choose a manufactured conservatory or use manufactured components in a custom-built conservatory. As specialists in these structures, conservatory manufacturers have developed combinations of materials and structural systems that solve the water problem. Manufactured conservatories also offer well-thought-out systems of climate control, including ventilation and supplemental heating and cooling, and they are available in a range of sizes and styles. ■

In its simplest form, a conservatory is not unlike a greenhouse, with walls and roof of glass and as little framework as possible. This metal-frame conservatory seems right at home even though its construction and details are very different from the clapboard house.

Plants provide privacy and shade for this porch as well as a lovely view from the chair.

A plant-filled conservatory is a joy year-round.

A Place for Plants

Porches, sunrooms, and conservatories provide opportunities for growing and displaying plants. Hanging baskets, pots, and window boxes full of colorful annuals adorn many porches from spring to fall. Because of all the glass, sunrooms and conservatories can be year-round plant rooms. If you're a serious gardener, a conservatory can serve as a live-in greenhouse, ideal for exotic plants such as orchids or for starting seeds for your summer garden in the dead of winter.

EXISTING WOODLAND
LAWN
PLANTER POCKET
LAWN
EXISTING DRIVEWAY
EXISTING WOODLAND
LAWN

CHAPTER 2

Design Practicalities

Whether you're adding or renovating a porch, three-season room, or sunroom, there are practical matters to consider before construction begins. Most importantly, each project has to abide by local building codes. And each project needs someone to do the work. In this chapter we'll walk through the ins and outs of regulations and offer some advice on finding a contractor who suits your needs and your temperament.

BUILDING CODES

Almost every community in the United States requires that structures, such as porches, erected within its jurisdiction be built to certain minimum standards set out in building codes. There are codes and regulations for every imaginable aspect of building, from the position of a structure on your property to the position of an electrical outlet in a wall. In addition to new structures, certain remodeling projects are also subject to code requirements. To ensure a project complies with the codes, towns and cities require building permits, obtained by presenting your plans to the town building department (or other agency). Technicians in the department will check that the plan's details—setbacks, structural loading, footing depth, wiring, and so on—pass muster.

Once construction begins, officials will make three or four separate inspections, including a footing inspection, a structural inspection for the framing, and if needed, separate electrical, plumbing, and heating/air conditioning inspections. At the end of the project, a final inspection ensures that the work has been properly completed.

Built at the same time as the rest of the house, this porch is covered in the building permits for the entire house.

Added on to an existing house, this sunroom must measure up to current codes and requires its own set of building permits.

Codes: Think Globally, Act Locally

Until 2000 there were dozens if not hundreds of major building codes in use around the world. After years of tinkering and discussion, the thousands of pages in the separate codes were finally distilled into the International Residential Code (IRC) and the International Building Code (IBC), for commercial work. Between them, these two codes cover safety, structural integrity, and access the world over—a formidable achievement.

That said, it doesn't make much sense to order a copy as a reference for your porch project. Not only are the books very thick and expensive, they might not cover everything your community requires. The IBC and IRC lay out minimum requirements; local jurisdictions may add or modify requirements. Always check with your local officials before you invest money in boards, bricks, and mortar.

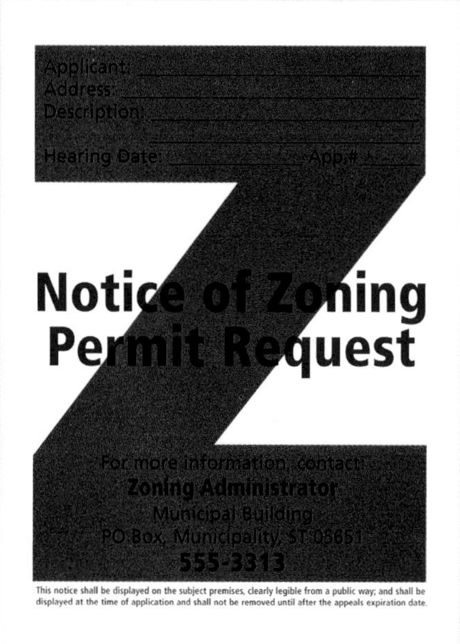
Applicant:
Address:
Description:
Hearing Date: App.#

Z

Notice of Zoning Permit Request

For more information, contact:
Zoning Administrator
Municipal Building
PO Box, Municipality, ST 08851
555-3313

This notice shall be displayed on the subject premises, clearly legible from a public way; and shall be displayed at the time of application and shall not be removed until after the appeals expiration date.

Manufacturers of three-season rooms, sunrooms (shown on this page), and conservatories strive to comply with the national building codes. Installers of these rooms must also make sure codes are followed, as is shown in the top photo in the beefed-up support structure needed to convert a deck to a sunroom.

Permits are not expensive, but homeowners and contractors often grumble about codes and their seemingly endless requirements. But codes help ensure that structures in your community withstand the test of time. (Some states require copies of building permits when doing title searches for refinancing or reselling.) They can also be a big help to you and your project. Knowledgeable people will make sure before you start construction that your design is technically sound—the foundation will support the posts, which will support the roof, which will withstand that heavy winter snow load. As work proceeds, inspections ensure that it is done properly, a good check if you're a do-it-yourselfer and useful encouragement to subcontractors to do their best.

Most permit processes also require a project to be completed in a certain amount of time. If you're doing it yourself, a deadline helps maintain forward momentum when mid-project malaise sets in. If you've subcontracted the work or hired a general contractor (as discussed later), the deadline gives you some official leverage if the work drags on.

Setbacks

Most towns have setback requirements that limit how close to the property line you can build. Setbacks can vary from the front to the

SMART TIP

Drawing Your Own Plans. In my city, the building department allows homeowners to draw up their own plans and obtain necessary permits based on those plans. Before you go very far in your design process, phone your building department and ask whether they allow homeowner-drawn plans or whether an architect's or engineer's plans are required. Some codes that allow homeowner-drawn plans require that an engineer or architect vouch for the plan's soundness (indicated by placing the state license stamp on the plan).

Restoring a porch like this to its original condition may not require permits. But it's best to check your local regulations before you start work on a restoration or renovation project.

Adding a sunroom to the end of a ranch house, as shown above and opposite, looks simple, but it can involve lots of planning to meet local zoning for property-line setbacks, building codes, and locating underground utilities before excavating the foundation.

> **SMART TIP**
>
> **Setback Caveat.** Setback distances for the side of a house that is adjacent to a road can be measured from different points depending on the zoning laws. The measurement may be from the centerline of the road, the edge of the pavement, or the edge of the town's right-of-way, which can be somewhere in your front yard. Make sure you check before making plans.

back of the house and from side to side. If you're planning to add a new porch or sunroom or to add onto an existing structure, one of the first things you should do is determine the setbacks on your property. This is important information. The city can require that all or part of a structure exceeding setbacks be torn down.

Less draconian solutions to setback violations exist, but they can be expensive, as I

Digging in the right place

If your project will require any digging (making new foundations or providing utilities, for example) you'll need to know whether there's anything down there you shouldn't be digging through, like power, gas, or sewer lines. The city doesn't want you to slice a line either, so they make it easy to find out where lines are—and it's a free service. Your codes department or the government pages of the phone directory will list the service and phone number. Usually within 48 hours of your call, the service will come out and set flags along the utility routes in your yard.

Buried services rarely interfere enough to require relocation or major reworking of a project, so you probably don't need to locate them during the design process. But you should make sure your builder has located them (particularly if you or a "moonlighting" friend in the construction trades are doing the building). And remember, the locator firms are not infallible; even when the flags are correctly placed, the utility they mark may be as much as 18 inches on either side of the flag line. Over the years, I've had guys cut into electric, gas, phone, and cable lines in unflagged and flagged areas. Cut electric and gas lines can cause considerable consternation; cut phone and cable lines are only an irritation but make for unhappy homeowners or neighbors.

Once service lines have been marked, footings can be dug safely (at least most of the time).

learned the hard way. In my town, the eaves (the portion of the roof that projects beyond the walls) of an addition must also fall within the setback requirements. After designing and building a sunroom addition for a townhouse, I discovered that one corner of an eave on the new sunroom projected a couple of inches into an adjacent property.

After surveying the lot, I found we could resolve the problem by transferring a strip about 18 inches wide from the adjacent lot to my client's lot. The neighbor was amenable to the transfer. He didn't even ask for payment; he just wanted the title to the property to be clear. But the bank balked, even though it owned the mortgages on both properties. It took hours of long-distance phone calls (the bank being part of a conglomerate with offices several states away) and several thousand dollars to complete the transfer.

So, do your homework in the planning phase of your project. If your project looks as if it will be derailed by a setback requirement, it is sometimes possible to obtain permission to push beyond the limits. Obtaining a variance from the planning or zoning board isn't easy, but planning and patience increase your chances. I once needed to extend a wall of a

SMART TIP

Meter Matters. If the location you like for your porch or sunroom includes the electrical service meter for your house, check with an electrician to find out whether the meter will have to be moved, which can be expensive.

Some three-season and sunroom projects produce very little disruption, top. Others provide considerable "opportunities" for relandscaping, bottom.

project about 2 feet beyond a 25-foot front-yard setback. Fortunately, this deviation would be barely noticeable when viewed from the street. I appealed to the zoning board for a variance. The request seemed reasonable, but most people think their requests are reasonable. I decided to leave nothing to chance. In addition to preparing plans and specifications, I talked to all the neighbors on both sides of the street. I explained what we proposed to do and asked them to sign a document indicating they had no objection to our plans. I also took pictures of the street and indicated on the pictures what impact the 2-foot projection would have. I submitted all this information well before the meeting. Of the seven variance requests on the table that day, mine was the only one approved.

You can find out the setback requirements for your property by checking with the codes office or with the city planning office. Setbacks are measured from the lot lines, which are established by the corners of your lot. Each corner is usually marked by a steel stake driven a few inches beneath the soil surface. In newer subdivisions it's usually easy to find the stakes. For an older house, you may

A porch addition like this one can be accomplished by an experienced home do-it-yourselfer. If you're not up to pouring concrete or shingling a roof, hire out those parts of the job and do the rest yourself.

need to rent a metal detector or hire an engineering or surveying firm to locate the stakes. This may cost several hundred dollars, but it's worth it if you're uncertain whether your porch or sunroom will come close to the setback limits.

DOING THE WORK

Most building projects, from erecting big buildings to adding onto a porch, involve two kinds of contractor. The general contractor (GC) organizes the entire job and is responsible to the owner/client for its successful completion. The actual work on the project is done by subcontractors who specialize in a building trade: concrete, framing, electrical, plumbing, roofing, and so on. The general contractor hires and is responsible for all the subcontractors on a project. The client, therefore, has to deal with only one person (or firm): the GC. A general contractor may also be a specialist; he or she may do all the carpentry on a job and subcontract the remainder of the work.

SMART TIP

The Fun Factor. My good friend and brother-in-law, a contractor in Santa Barbara, California, decided after a particularly difficult quarter that he would take only jobs that were both profitable and fun. That's a very good rule, advantageous to both the contractor and the client. If you can't imagine yourself having a laugh or at least a smile with a potential contractor, keep looking.

Painted details make something special of this simple screened porch. Earmark a little money in your budget for finishing touches.

Custom-made windows installed decades ago effected an elegant transformation of this porch to three-season room.

A general contractor can coordinate building and landscaping work so your property goes from job site to showpiece, like the three-season room shown at left, as quickly as possible.

There is no requirement to employ a general contractor. Homeowners frequently serve as their own GC on remodeling projects, perhaps doing part of the work themselves while hiring and supervising subcontractors for the rest. Before you decide to serve as your own general contractor, give some thought to what the job entails. A general contractor is not unlike a conductor directing an orchestra to bring a symphony to life. With skillful direction, the orchestra makes beautiful music, sometimes loud, sometimes soft, with all the various players coming in at just the right time. Under a poor conductor, however, the orchestra produces only noise and confusion.

This house may or may not have had a porch in its past, but this handsome addition looks like it has always been there.

You may save some money acting as your own GC, but unless you're experienced in construction, there are several very good reasons to hire a professional. A competent general contractor will be familiar with all aspects of the process and will be able to make sure the work is done correctly. An experienced general contractor will know who the best subcontractors are for your project. I've done a lot of general contracting, and I've used many of the same subcontractors for years. I know them and most of their help, so I know who will be working on the job. My subs know that I expect quality work and professional behavior. As a general contractor, I make sure the client doesn't have to deal with loud radios, parking problems, tire tracks in the sand box, or stevedore language.

The most difficult part of any project is keeping the work flowing smoothly so that the job is finished on time. Even experienced general contractors won't always have a seamless work flow, but they have some significant advantages over nonprofessionals in keeping things moving. They've done this before, lots of times. They understand the rhythm of the job, knowing when to push and when to ease off, and when to schedule the electrician or the carpenter. Most importantly, general contractors have a relationship with their subs. They've likely worked together for years and may meet for coffee at the local watering hole. If the sub is really busy, but the GC needs him or her on a certain day, the sub will try to work out the schedule to help the GC.

Complicated additions, like this two-story sunroom, require coordination between a number of subcontractors for on-time, efficient construction.

The gable end of this sunroom addition fits seamlessly with the existing gabled house. Connections to the existing structure have been carefully planned and executed, including special flashing to divert water from a vulnerable point of intersection.

An imaginative, skilled contractor can add interesting touches to a project. The details shown above go a step beyond the ordinary in design or execution.

Choosing a Contractor

Because I'm a contractor, I can't claim objectivity on this topic. Nevertheless, many years spent working with clients and, in particular, choosing subcontractors to do work for me have given me some insights that I hope will be useful.

First, you should be comforted to know that in most places, dishonest or unethical contractors don't stay in business very long. The community of tradespeople is not large, and word soon gets out about how a person conducts his or her business. I may get taken once by an incompetent or unsavory subcontractor, but I won't be taken twice.

So, do some investigating, talk to people. If you're looking for a general contractor, talk to subcontractors who work with the GC you're considering. Check with the Better Business Bureau to see whether there are complaints on file. Find out whether the contractor is a member of trade organizations such as the National Association of Homebuilders (NAHB) or the Remodelers Council of NAHB. Look at completed jobs, and ask the owners about their experiences with the

A porch renovation often presents opportunities for other amenities, such as this porch-deck combination. Contracting for both at once can save money.

You and your contractor will need to plan ahead to accommodate all materials the project may require. Materials for a smaller project may be delivered all at once, left. Those for a big project will likely come in stages, bottom left.

When you're choosing a contractor, ask previous clients how well the crews cleaned up. Construction makes a mess, and interior and exterior work sites should be cleaned daily, as shown in the photos opposite, so debris doesn't get traipsed all over your house.

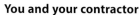

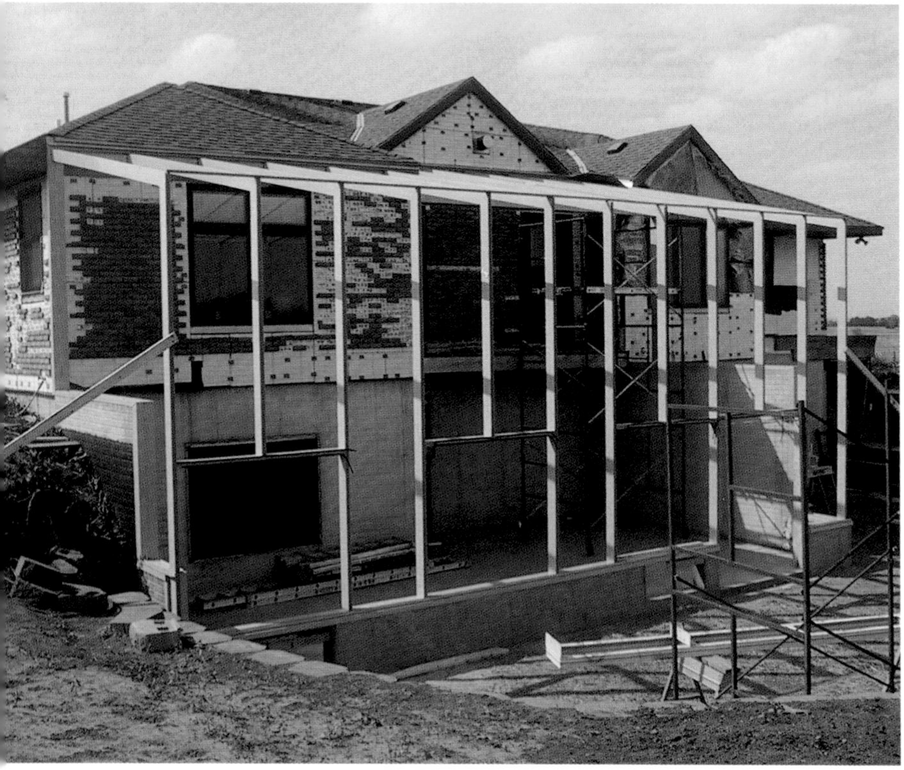

GC or subcontractor. Listen to what they say, but listen fairly. Every contractor has had jobs go wrong, and not always because he or she was unethical or incompetent. The conditions necessary for a "perfect storm" can occur in any business.

When you consider price, remember that contractors are in business to make money. If you look only for the lowest bid, expect the lowest quality job—a profit has to be squeezed out of that low bid somehow.

In addition to objective criteria, meet with the contractor to see whether this is a person you want to share your life with for the duration of a remodeling project. I know this is subjective, but there's something to be said for gut feelings. Over the years I've

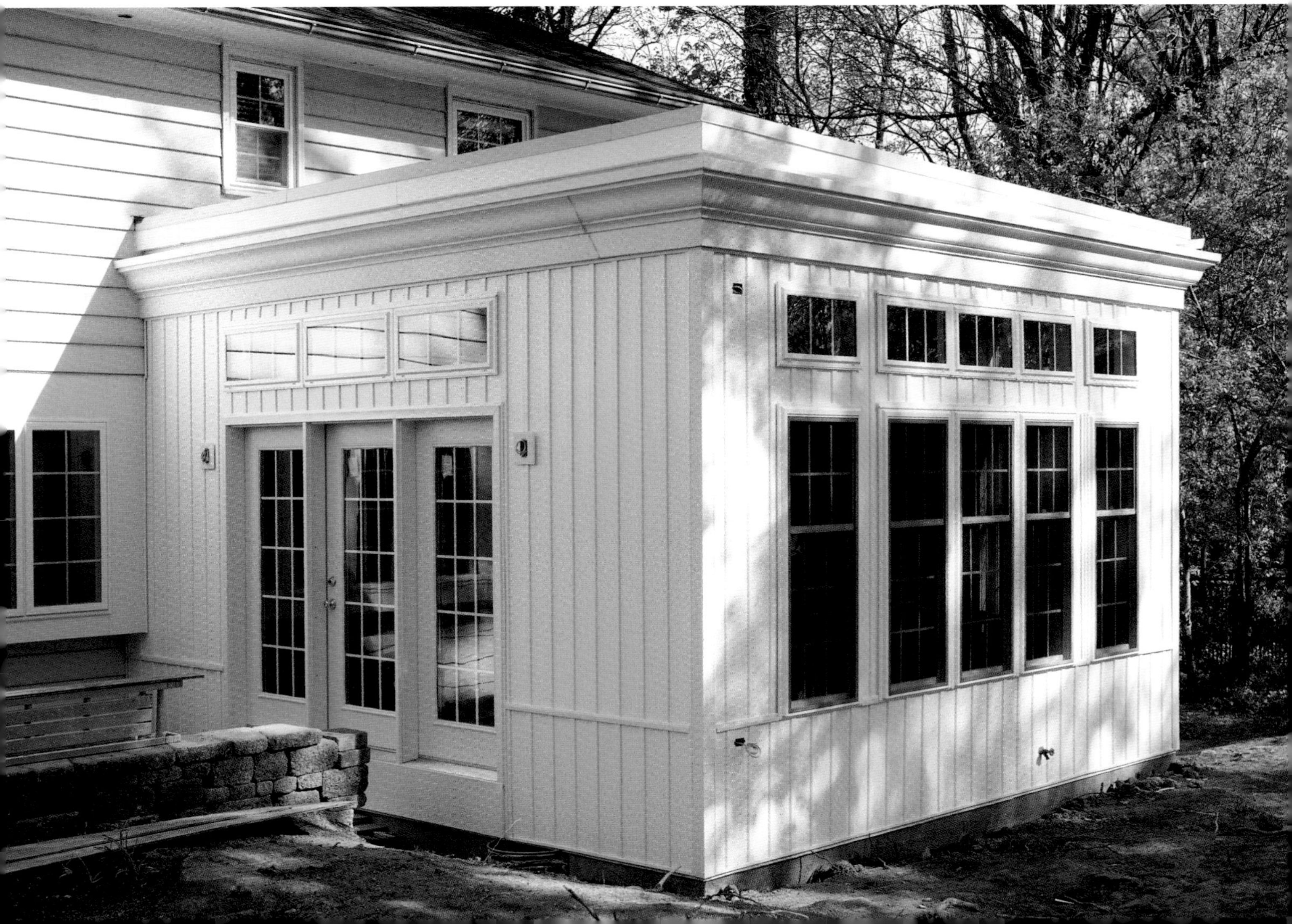

learned that if I'm uncomfortable when interviewing prospective clients, I should pass up the job. You should do the same with a contractor who makes you uneasy. Adding or remodeling a porch or sunroom is stressful; you're changing things, tearing down something old and familiar and replacing it with something new and unfamiliar. When you're up to your eyeballs in dust, demolition, and dirt, it's important to have a good relationship with your contractor.

If yours is a steep site like the one shown on this page, find a contractor with experience working in these conditions, which can pose difficulties in construction as well as access.

GAINING ACCESS

Before committing to a location for the porch or sunroom, think about access. I don't mean how the addition fits into the traffic patterns people follow in and around your house (which you should have already considered), but how the backhoe can get into the backyard to dig the foundations or how the lumberyard truck is going to deliver the roof trusses.

Access limitations may pose such major headaches that you'll have to rethink your design or your location. More often, providing access is less problematic. Fences may need to be removed or relocated; shrubs and even trees occasionally need to be dug up. There is usually some damage to repair. The backhoe may need to drive through your perennial garden. Sidewalks, patios, or driveways may be cracked by the weight of heavy equipment and need repair or replacement.

Thinking of access sooner rather than later will allow you to plan the most convenient and least damaging access routes and to anticipate the costs of moving, replacing, or repairing things that are in the way. An experienced general contractor should consider access and account for its costs in his or her bid. You can't anticipate all the damage that may occur. Take note of existing conditions before construction begins. As a contractor, I take pictures before every job so the homeowner and I have some objective way of determining whether the gutters were damaged during the course of the work or before work began. ■

Before you commit to a design or a contractor, make sure that it will be possible to move necessary equipment onto the site. In the wooded area shown above, compact equipment solved the problem. At the beach, below, there was plenty of room to build a screened porch.

CHAPTER 3

Open-Air Porches

Few simple pleasures have the restorative power of a couple of hours spent resting in a comfortable chair on a porch. Add a good friend and a glass of wine, or a good book and a gentle breeze, and life doesn't get much better. While porches of all shapes, sizes, and styles will deliver this reward, each has its own character and its own practical requirements. This chapter looks at the basic elements of porch structure as well as at those little touches that can make your porch special.

Grand or modest, porches have a special place in our sense of what makes a house a home.

A LOOK BACK

The simplest porch evokes an image of the old west, with a straight shed roof on two posts over a low plank deck. Those porches hearken back to a Caribbean style of building, which may itself borrow from African influences, brought to the American South by the human cargo of the slave traders. Other southern porches derive from French Norman and Neo-Classical styles, in which an extension of the roof covers a wide veranda, or from the Spanish Colonial house, in which a balcony porch extends out over the ground floor. The Greek Revival porches on Southern mansions were mostly for show, impressing visitors with enormous columns and a towering elevation, while the less formal "sitting porch" on the second floor was more inviting.

Flowers and colorful paint greatly enhance this modest porch.

Porches have a long history in the Southwest, where they offer respite from the ever-present sun.

The high gabled roof, exposed beams, and sturdy brick piers of this Arts and Crafts-style porch, left, dominate the house facade. Much daintier, with its thin posts, filigreed brackets, and lower profile, the porch below adds an equally distinctive, if not dominant, touch to its house.

Long absent from contemporary architecture, porches are making a comeback on new houses. The handsome wood-shingled porch and house opposite are a fully integrated design.

But the porch came into its own in American architecture with the advent of "stick style" house framing and machine-made intricate brackets and balustrades in the 1840s and '50s. Architect Andrew Jackson Downing wrote pattern books linking the American house to the landscape through porches and was instrumental in making the porch a seminal part of the American experience. It's interesting that porches were a reactionary backlash to the very machinery and industrialization that made them affordable and therefore ubiquitous. This back-to-nature movement in design reflected the literary and social call of Ralph Waldo Emerson and Henry David Thoreau.

Whatever you desire from your porch here in the twenty-first century, from simple to complex, all porches share three basic characteristics: a deck, posts or columns, and a roof. That's really all there is to it. But those three elements combine in myriad ways.

Supports for Elevated Porch Decks

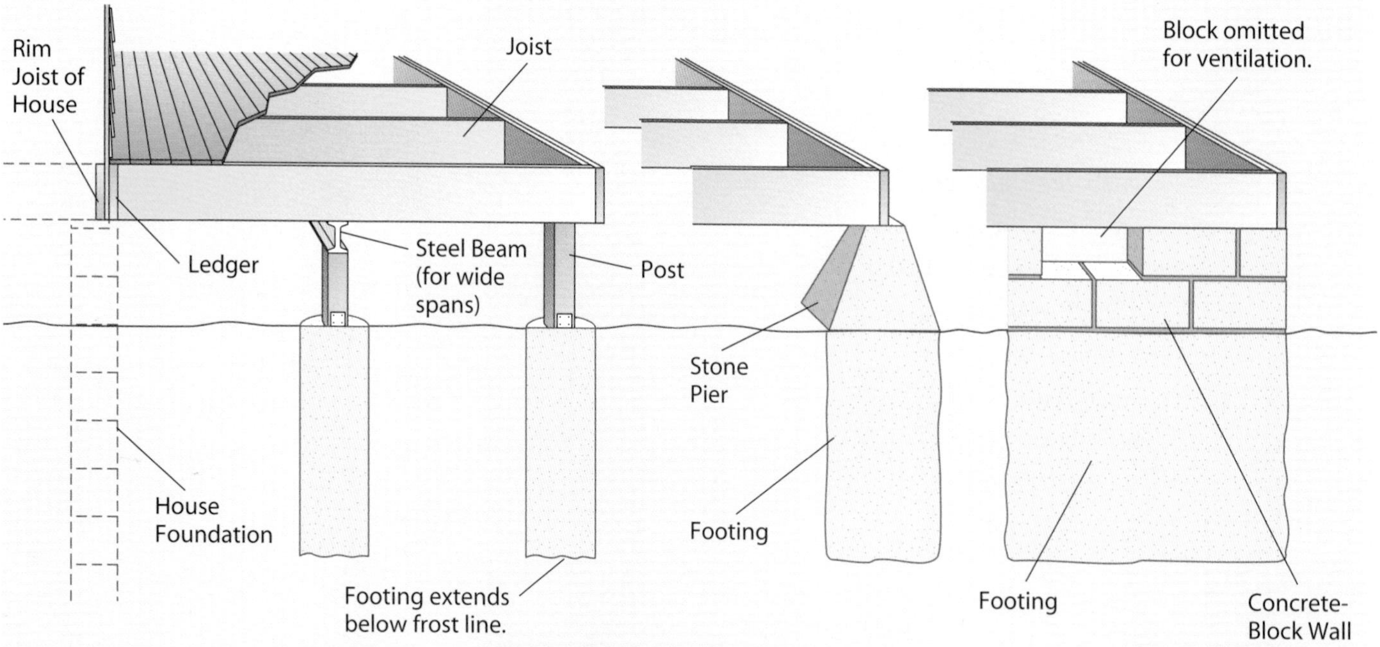

Ground-to-roof piers support the roof of this stuccoed porch.

A concrete-block pier supports the deck and posts of this porch.

A stone wall and railing-height pier underpin this substantial porch.

THE DECK

When many people think of the deck, or floor, of a porch, they picture a surface several feet off the ground reached by a handsome set of steps. Elevated porch decks are common because they suit many popular house styles. In the north, an elevated deck also raises porch sitters above a layer of cold air that hugs the ground in cool or cold weather. But where temperatures are warm year-round, there's a history of ground-level porch decks that developed with Spanish- and Mediterranean-style houses. I'll discuss elevated decks first.

Elevated decks are supported above the ground by posts, piers, or walls. Posts are commonly made of wood or steel. Piers are essentially masonry posts made of poured concrete, block, stone, or brick. Walls can be framed of wood or made of masonry. All of these supports can be embellished with moldings and other decorative elements.

Posts, piers, and walls must themselves be supported by footings in the ground that prevent the supports from sinking into the soil or, in cold-winter climates, moving with the expansion and contraction of freezing and thawing soil. Today, codes specify the depth and composition of footings for porch posts, piers, and walls, just as they do for the footings underpinning a house. In the past, however, porch footings were often left up to the discretion of the builder.

In Nebraska, where today's footings must extend below the frost line (at least 3 feet deep), I've worked on old porches with footings that were little more than a course or two of limestone or a layer of concrete a few inches deep. Needless to say, these old porches often slumped or leaned. In warm

Raised porches are common where winters are cold.

Attaching a New Porch to a House

A solid attachment of a new porch to the existing house is critical: the fasteners must carry the load of the deck at that point. Consequences can be serious if they fail. A few years ago a deck in my town that had only been nailed to the house came loose from its moorings during a party. Fortunately, no one was seriously injured, but the people on the deck took a harrowing ride to the ground.

The drawings show deck-support fastenings secured to two different house facades. For a wood-frame house with a facade of stucco, clapboard, or vinyl siding, I remove the existing siding and lag-screw the porch ledger through the sub-siding into the skirt board, drawing the ledger tight to the framing of the house. (Though stucco looks quite solid, it isn't made to carry a load; it must be cut away like wood siding.) If the entire porch deck is exposed to rain, I install flashing under the siding and over the decking to keep the ledger from getting wet and rotting. If the porch is deep or the climate isn't rainy, this isn't necessary.

On a masonry house (brick, block, stone, or stucco over block), I attach the ledger with masonry fasteners that are long enough to engage the structural masonry—the brick or stone veneer or the block behind the stucco facing, for example. The fasteners are sized according to load and to the quality and hardness of the masonry.

Attaching a New Porch

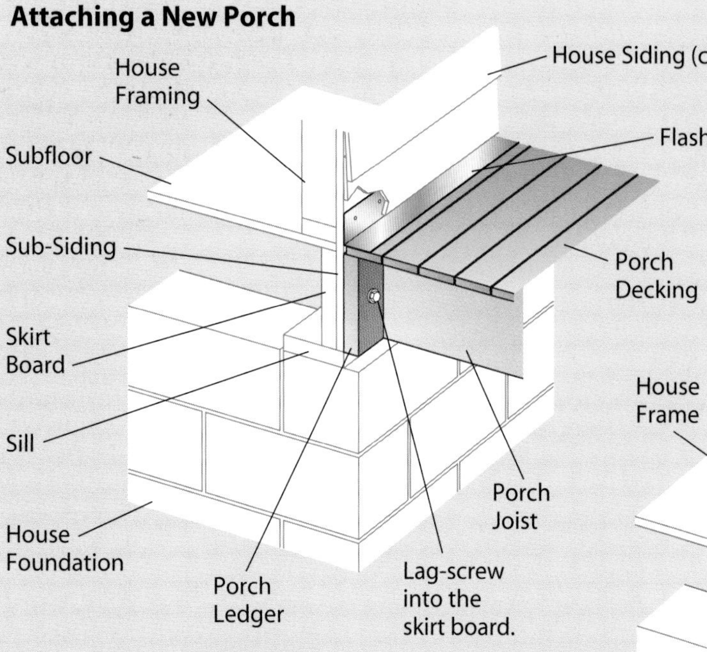

Frame House

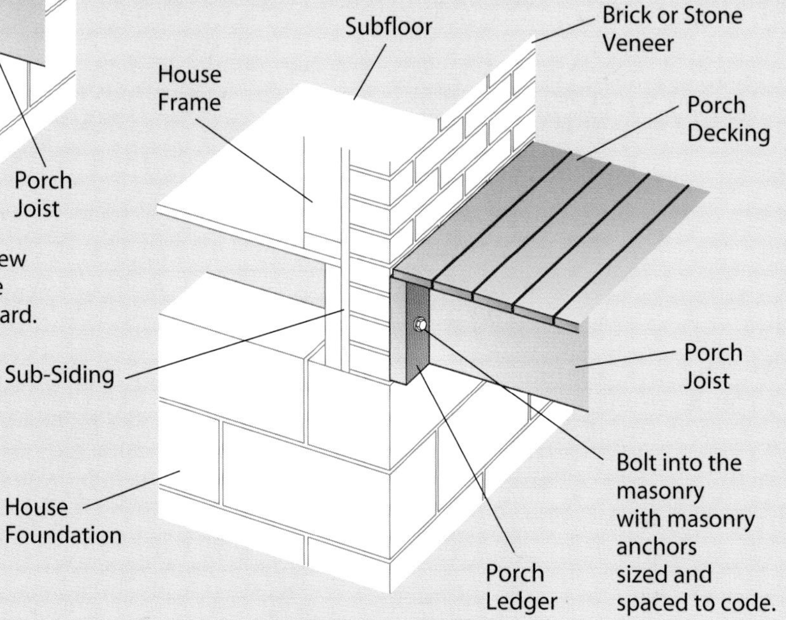

Masonry House

climates, old porch footings are sometimes no more than firmly tamped earth or a large stone underneath each post. With little soil moisture and freeze-thaw movement to counter, some of these footings hold up remarkably well.

Deck Substructure

Like the floor of a house, the deck of an elevated porch is supported by joists, which rest on the posts, piers, or walls. Joists are usually made of wood sized according to code to accommodate the span and load of the deck and its occupants. (For wide spans, steel beams sometimes provide additional support.) Open to the elements, elevated decks must slope away from the house so that rainwater drains away from the foundation. The usual slope is a drop of ¼ inch per foot.

SMART TIP

Lasting Joists. Codes specify that wooden joists less than 18 inches above the ground must be treated with a preservative or be a type of wood naturally resistant to decay, such as cedar or redwood. (If the joists rest on the ground, they must be rated Ground Contact.) Today, wood is most often treated for water and pest resistance with ACQ (shorthand for its active ingredient, alkaline copper quaternary). ACQ replaces chromated copper arsenate (CCA), which raised concern for residential use due to its arsenic content.

For joists more than 18 inches above the ground, codes allow you to use common framing lumber, called SPF (spruce/pine/fir). But the codes also require that wood exposed to the weather be treated. Technically, if you cover the joists with painted decking, you've protected the joists from the weather. However, in my experience, water eventually penetrates decking. I suggest you take the long view and spend a little more for joists that won't deteriorate.

This two-story porch suits the site and architecture.

Deck Fasteners

Porch decking, like most residential wood flooring, is usually nailed in place. Tongue-and-groove pine can be blind nailed, as shown in the drawing, so that the nail heads aren't visible. Face-nailed or face-screwed decking is less elegant but cheaper to install. Screws are more expensive than nails, but they don't loosen over time as nails tend to do. Because they're exposed to the weather, deck nails and screws (even blind nails) should be galvanized or otherwise treated to prevent rust. If you choose cedar for decking, be aware that almost all fasteners, treated or not, tend to stain the wood. Stainless-steel fasteners are reputed not to stain cedar, but I've seen them leave some discoloration.

Galvanized fasteners are dipped in a zinc bath; some are "hot-dipped" for use with lumber treated with ACQ, which eats right through ordinary galvanized fasteners. Other treated fasteners include GRK Fasteners' Climatek-treated screws (which are gold-colored screws), or Prime Guard Plus (a green-colored screw.).

If you aren't installing tongue-and-groove material, you can still get a fastener-free deck surface by using a metal-bracket fastening system such as Shadoe Track or Tiger Claw. (Many of the composite manufacturers offer similar systems with their products.) As the drawing shows, the brackets are attached to the joists and then to the underside of the decking.

Traditional pine tongue-and-groove porch decking is blind-nailed, which protects the boards from rotting and looks good, too.

Nailing Floor Boards

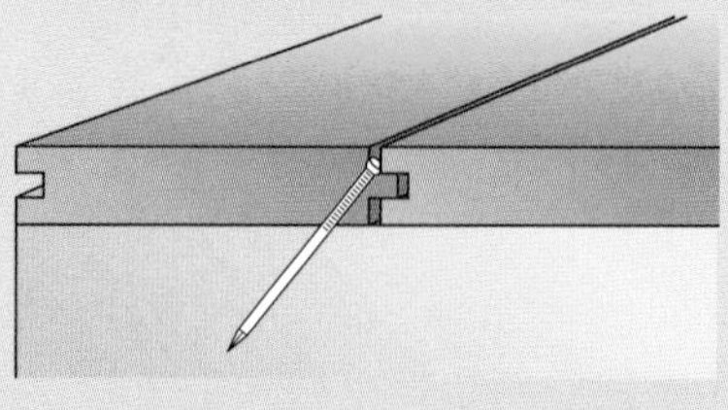

Blind-nailed Tongue-and-Groove Floor

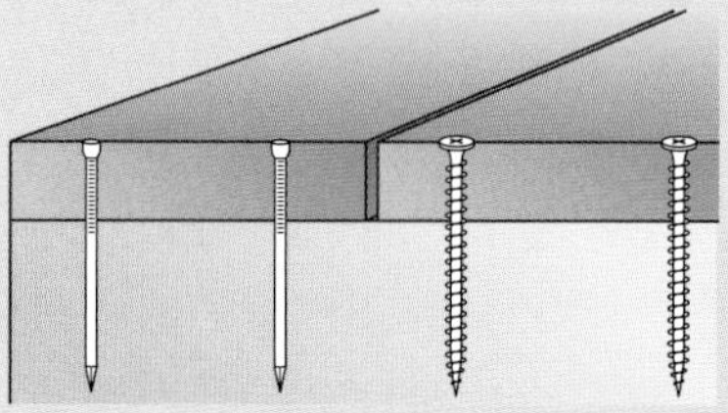

Face-nailed or Screwed Butt-jointed Floor

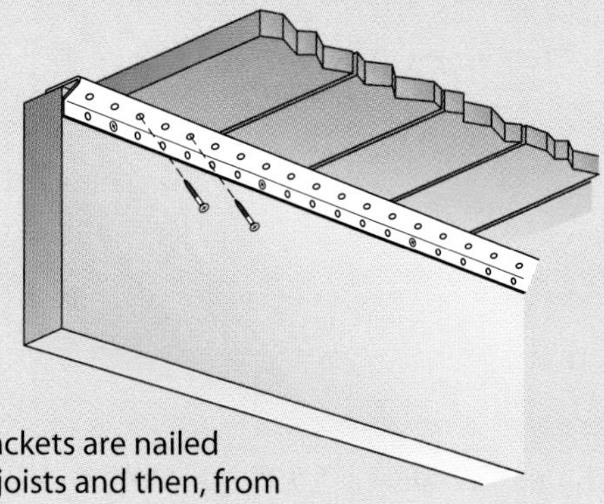

Brackets are nailed to joists and then, from underneath, to floor boards.

Hidden Brackets

Deck Materials

Other than your style preferences, the main considerations for porch decking are durability and weather resistance. There are more decking options today than the tongue-and-groove pine boards widely used into the 1950s. Inexpensive and durable, tongue-and-groove pine 1×4s were often installed perpendicular to the house facade, so water would run down the joints along the slope away from the house. Blind nailed and then painted, pine decking stood up well to the weather. (See "Deck Fasteners," opposite, for more on blind nailing.)

Years ago, good-quality pine milled for flooring contained few knots and was often cut with the growth rings perpendicular to the board faces. These quartersawn, or vertical-grain, boards hold up much better to the wear and tear of traffic than the "flat sawn" material common today. Vertical-grain pine is still available. It's not cheap, but it is worth the extra money if you're set on traditional flooring. It also looks lovely under a clear, tough exterior varnish.

Other wood-flooring possibilities include a variety of naturally rot-resistant woods. Cedar, redwood, and cypress are domestic softwoods commonly used as decking for open-air decks. They are softer and less durable than vertical-grain pine, but they're certainly acceptable for porch decking. Of imported woods, teak is a beautiful, durable, and very expensive option. In recent years other imports have gained favor for decks and porches. (See "Smart Tip," right.) Treated domestic softwood lumber can also be used as decking material; it's the least attractive but also the least expensive choice.

Woods that resist decay do not need to be painted. Unfinished, they weather to a silvery

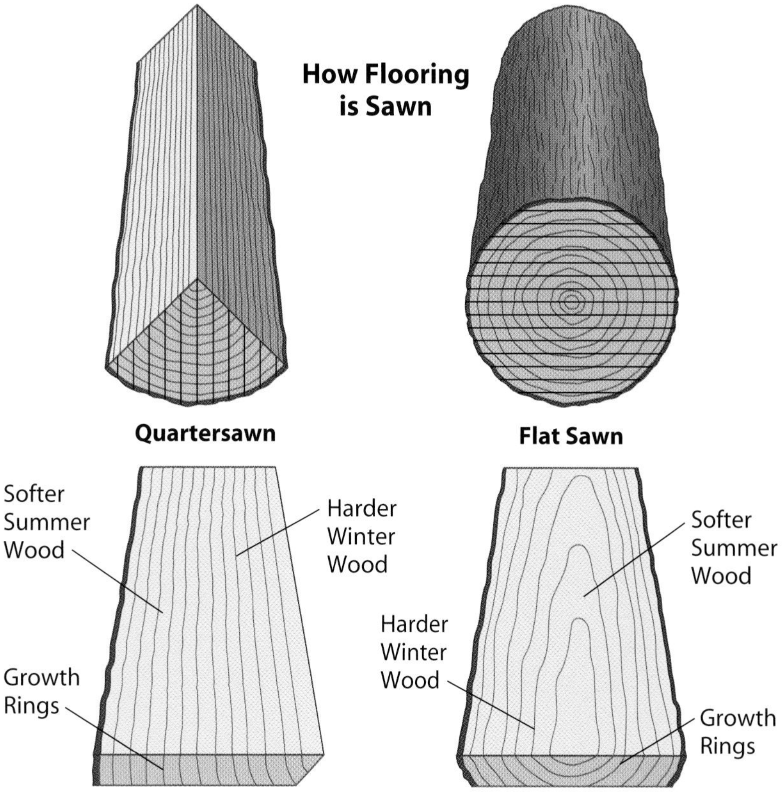

Quartersawn flooring wears better than flat-sawn flooring because it has more hard winter wood on its faces.

SMART TIP

Exotic Lumber. Attractive, durable, weather- and pest-resistant imported, or exotic, hardwoods are increasingly available for use as outdoor flooring. Ipe, a Brazilian import, has been in use for 30 years. It is extraordinarily durable and resistant to fire, moisture, insects, decay, fungi, and termites. Like the much costlier teak, ipe has striking color and grain patterns that can be preserved by a clear finish. Left unfinished, ipe, like most woods, weathers to a silvery gray.

A number of other exotics have similar qualities but are less widely available. Exotics can be difficult to locate simply because they have dozens of common names. Before deciding on an exotic, find out how long it has been used as an exterior flooring in North America—those with more history are likely to have suffered fewer problems.

A brick or tile porch deck is best laid on a concrete base, which can be poured on an elevated deck with properly reinforced supports, right.

A brightly colored rug adds a little zing to the rustic flooring of this mountain deck, below.

The painted tongue-and-groove deck on the classic porch shown opposite pairs effectively with the clear-finished ceiling boards.

gray. If you want to keep their distinctive coloring, you can varnish or treat them with a penetrating sealer. Those sealers sold as "protective" usually include chemicals to prevent mildew and algae growth and deterioration from ultraviolet light.

Many substantial old houses feature porches with elevated decks of poured concrete. (An acquaintance of mine has torn down a number of these over the years and has found bedsprings and other peculiar stuff embedded in the slabs as reinforcement.) Concrete remains a wonderfully weather-resistant and durable option today, even though it requires a beefed up substructure to carry the weight. If you're interested in a ceramic tile or stone surface, concrete is a necessary substrate. It isn't a good idea to lay tile or stone on a wood deck, even one prepared with ½-inch cement board over a ¾-inch plywood base. The deck

This beautifully restored house displays how important an elaborate porch was to the Victorian style.

Deck Painting: A Lesson Learned

Wooden porch decks can suffer a lot of wear and tear, so it pays to be conscientious when painting or varnishing them. I always use the recommended primer for paint or varnish and follow instructions on the number of primer and top coats. On one porch, I decided to go even further and "back prime" all the decking boards—that is, prime all the surfaces of the boards before nailing them in place. I thought this might add to the life of the deck. It had the opposite effect. In just a couple of years, the boards split, twisted, warped, and decayed, and we had to replace most of the deck.

Why this happened is still not clear to me. My best guess is that moisture penetrated the finish despite our efforts, and because the entire surface was painted, the wood couldn't dry out. Since then, I've laid unfinished decking and then primed and painted it. Looking at old porches, this seems to be the way tongue-and-groove porch decking has always been finished. I guess the old guys knew what they were doing.

Composite flooring, above, can be difficult to distinguish from its wooden counterpart.

Painted gray, the boards of the pine deck at right are laid so water will drain away from the house along the joints.

Face-nailed, wide-plank decking left unfinished to weather adds to the rustic and somewhat eccentric character of a log-cabin porch, below.

is still likely to flex enough to crack the grout between the tiles, eventually allowing water to penetrate to the floor joists, which would rot over time.

Composite boards made of recycled plastic and wood, ground up and reconstituted, are relatively recent options for porch decking. Durable and weather resistant, composite materials require little maintenance other than the occasional scrub.

The price of flooring fluctuates regularly and varies considerably among different materials. Here are some useful comparisons. Treated wood is the least expensive. Tongue-and-groove pine and cedar are usually about double the cost of treated wood. Composite

material is almost four times as expensive as treated material. Installation costs are similar for most of the materials, though blind nailing tongue-and-groove flooring takes more time than face nailing, as does installing metal-bracket systems. When comparing costs, however, be sure to factor in the cost of finishing raw wood with paint, varnish, or penetrating sealer, and the cost of long-term maintenance. Materials that cost more initially may compare favorably over the long haul.

As it matures this planting will enhance the entry as well as serve as a skirting for the porch.

A simple square lattice skirting can be playful or formal, depending on the setting and choice of colors.

Deck Skirting

The area beneath a raised deck is an awkward space. Usually less than 3 or 4 feet high, it is too cramped to provide useful storage. If you're supporting the deck on posts or piers, the openings between them can look ugly and quickly become uglier with the clutter of paper, leaves, and other debris that soon collects there (not to mention the critters that set up housekeeping under the porch). Some sort of screening enhances the look of the porch and saves an uncomfortable crawling

This porch's baluster and skirting areas, above, are covered in clapboard to match the house siding. The attractive cutout provides ventilation.

The skirting shown at left echoes the simple balusters above it.

This interesting combination of slanted and vertical lattice, below, was made by the homeowner, as was the attractive baluster.

Gaps in the stone foundation ventilate the area under the porch above.

Poured concrete is commonly used for ground-level porch decks, opposite. Here, concrete is combined with paving bricks laid on a solid base.

cleanup every few months. Whatever screening you choose, make sure you allow plenty of air flow to prevent condensation from rotting the decking.

Lattice panels and picket fencing are commonly used. Shrubs block off the area visually, but unless they are very dense, they won't stop debris from finding its way through. An attractive solution, particularly for large masonry porches, is a gridwork screen of large sandstone or concrete blocks. Make sure you set them on a solid footing. I've repaired old porches where such blocks were laid without frost footings, and seasonal soil movement tipped and skewed them.

Ground-Level Porch Decks

A ground-level deck surface can be as simple as tamped earth or as elaborate as an intricate pattern of ceramic tile laid on a concrete slab. Climate and the degree of formality you desire are the main factors in choosing a ground-level surface. The most common is a concrete slab, which is a durable option for any climate and a wide range of house styles. The concrete itself can serve as a finished surface, or it can be stamped with decorative patterns. It can also serve as a substrate for ceramic tile, paver, or stone.

Where freeze-thaw cycles occur, a concrete slab often needs proper footings. Footings may not be required around the entire perimeter, but they are necessary under any load-bearing posts or walls that rest on the slab and under walls that are attached to the house. If you plan to use an existing slab, make sure it has the necessary footings or that they can be added.

Peeled tree trunks and bold, simple capitals support this Southwestern porch roof, left.

Doric columns, such as those below, serve the same function for this porch as they did on Greek temples constructed 2,500 years ago.

Shingle-clad columns, right, blend into the house facade and support a room above this porch.

POSTS & COLUMNS

Functionally, posts and columns support the porch roof. They can rest on the deck and extend to the roof rafters, or they can extend from the footings to the roof while supporting the deck along the way.

A porch roof usually doesn't require much to hold it up—a few 4×4s will often do the job. But a bare 4×4 doesn't look like much. So, long ago, structural efficiency gave way to visual interest. Today, a wonderfully

This renovated porch is supported on wooden posts that run from the ground to the roof.

Columns in every classical style are found on old and new porches, left.

These airy metal posts, below, make a small porch seem larger.

varied array of designs and embellishments gives porch posts and columns character.

For Victorian-style porches, posts not much more substantial than a 4×4 are faceted or rounded and topped with fretwork and filigree brackets. In the Southwest, massive timbers support clay-tiled roofs. In the mountains, tree trunks stripped of their bark help marry porches to log-built homes. Bungalow porches everywhere feature substantial-looking columns clad in boards, siding, or stucco to match the trim or facade of the house. Stone or brick piers anchor porches on stately masonry homes. And columns in classical Greek, Roman, or Egyptian styles (or any number of fanciful derivatives) lend a distinctive look to a wide range of porches.

Post Practicalities

The drawings below show common porch post and column constructions. A wooden post at ground level should be fixed to a raised portion of the footing or on a pier block. The deck structure and roof then attach to the post along its length.

> **SMART TIP**
>
> **Post Support.** A post for a porch (or any structure attached to the house) should never be sunk into a hole, even one dug deeper than the frost line. Instead, it should rest on top of a code-approved footing or foundation. Even rot-resistant or treated wood will deteriorate over time when buried in the ground. I've seen cedar fences leaning precipitously where the posts were set in solid concrete and were rotted off at ground level. Furthermore, a 4x4 or 6x6 post lacks the surface-bearing area to carry a roof load, let alone that of an entire porch.

Post and Column Construction

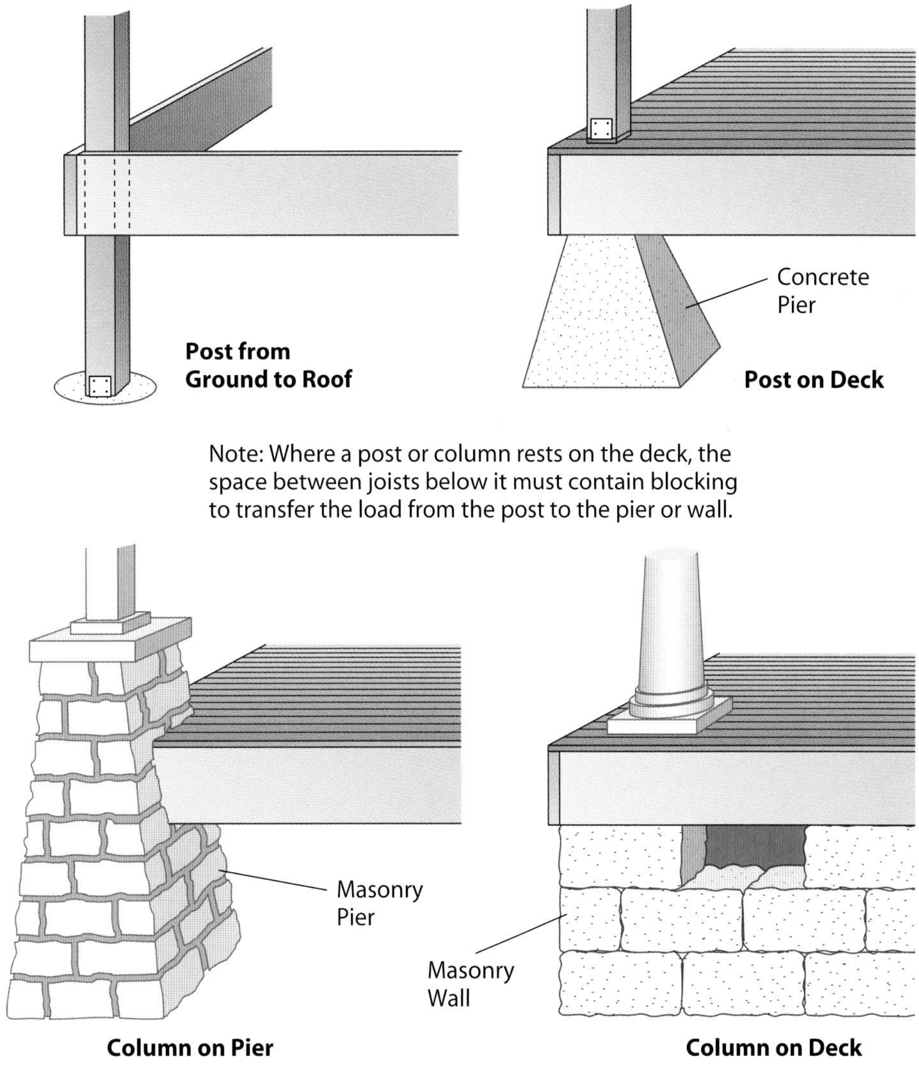

The enclosure for the porch shown above, made by forming graceful arched openings in the brick walls, forms a seamless facade with the rest of the house. The masonry posts shown below run from the ground to the roof, providing attractive and effective porch support.

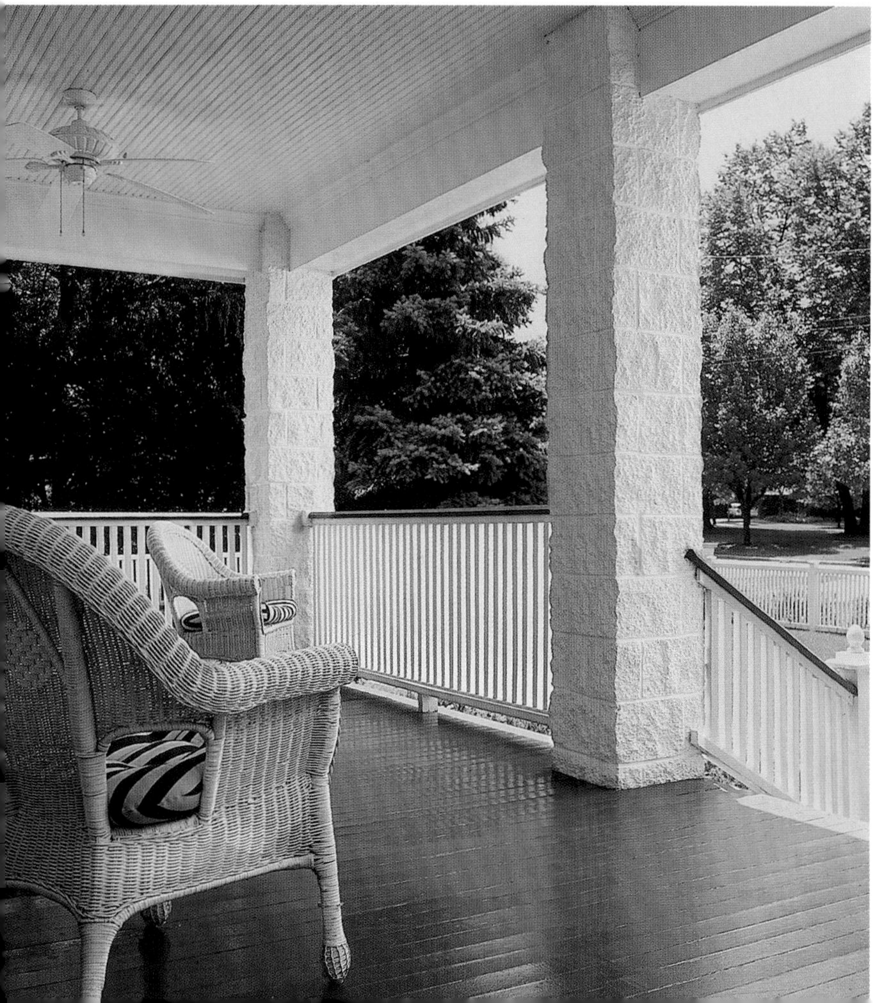

On some porches, masonry walls extend from the foundation to railing height above the deck. Shorter posts or columns rest on the walls to support the roof. Masonry piers can do the same, with wooden or cast-stone railings stretched between the piers. The pier can also extend to the roof. Masonry walls and piers are made from a great range of materials, including river rock, rough or cut quarried stone, brick, or decorative cast-concrete blocks. Walls and piers may have plumb vertical lines or may taper upward from a wide base. Some are built entirely

The square columns of this porch are supported by a bearing wall that doubles as a railing.

of masonry. Others are framed of wood with a masonry veneer. Cast-stone newel posts, balusters, and railings often complement masonry designs.

Placing posts or columns on top of the deck rather than extending them up from the footings allows more freedom of design. You can use simple treated posts or masonry to support the deck, hiding them with skirting. Then you can treat the above-deck posts and columns as you wish.

Posts and columns can be made of wood, fiberglass, metal, cast stone, or composite

Here a poured concrete porch deck and piers are clad with faux-stone veneer. Plywood encloses a post supporting the roof. The plywood will itself be covered with a wood or vinyl skin.

A pilaster against the wall, above left, complements this column.

A massive cast-stone column gives the shallow porch shown above right a presence that a thinner column would not.

materials. They can be square, faceted, round, or a combination of shapes. Adding a base and capital, decorative moldings, or braces can transform a plain post at relatively little cost. If your taste runs to the classical, columns in Tuscan, Doric, Ionic, Corinthian, and Composite styles are available in wood, cast stone, and fiberglass.

If wood sounds like too much trouble, you can buy posts and columns made of a variety of more-weatherproof materials. Stone, cast iron, and steel have long been available, but they can expensive options. Cast stone, fiberglass, and composite materials offer a range of styles at prices affordable to more people. Cast stone provides the look

Creating Columns

Perhaps more than any other single element, decorative columns make a porch distinctive. Available in a wide range of styles, columns can be structural and bear the weight of the roof. Or they can be ornamental, encasing a structural support. Structural columns usually come in one piece; decorative columns come in halves that must be fastened around the support on site. Decorative columns are made of traditional materials, such as wood, stone, iron, or steel, as well as fiberglass, cast stone, and a variety of composites.

A wooden post or column may be solid—a tree trunk stripped of its bark or a solid timber ranging from a 4x4 to massive pieces 18 inches or more square. Solid posts and columns are prone to splitting along their length during their initial curing or as a result of seasonal absorption and loss of moisture. Such defects can enhance the rustic look of certain styles, but they are not welcome on a Victorian post or a classical column. To eliminate splitting, wooden columns can be glued up of individual staves (much like those of a barrel). Round stave-built columns are turned on a giant lathe after assembly. Whether solid or stave-built, wooden posts and columns can last a long time if properly painted or varnished.

Cross Section of Turned Column

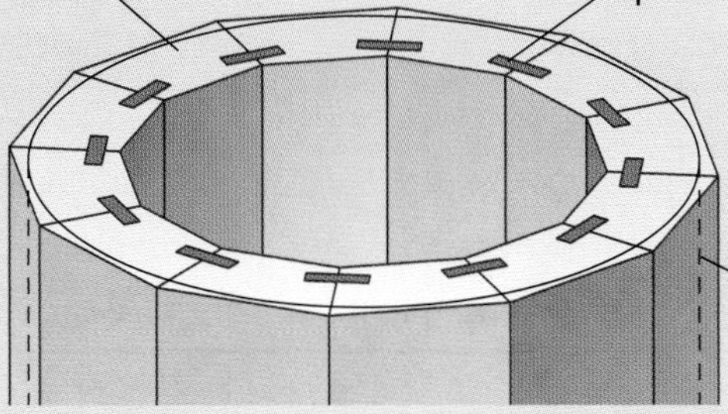

After assembly, the column is turned on a lathe; a dotted line indicates the turned face.

Porch Column Anatomy

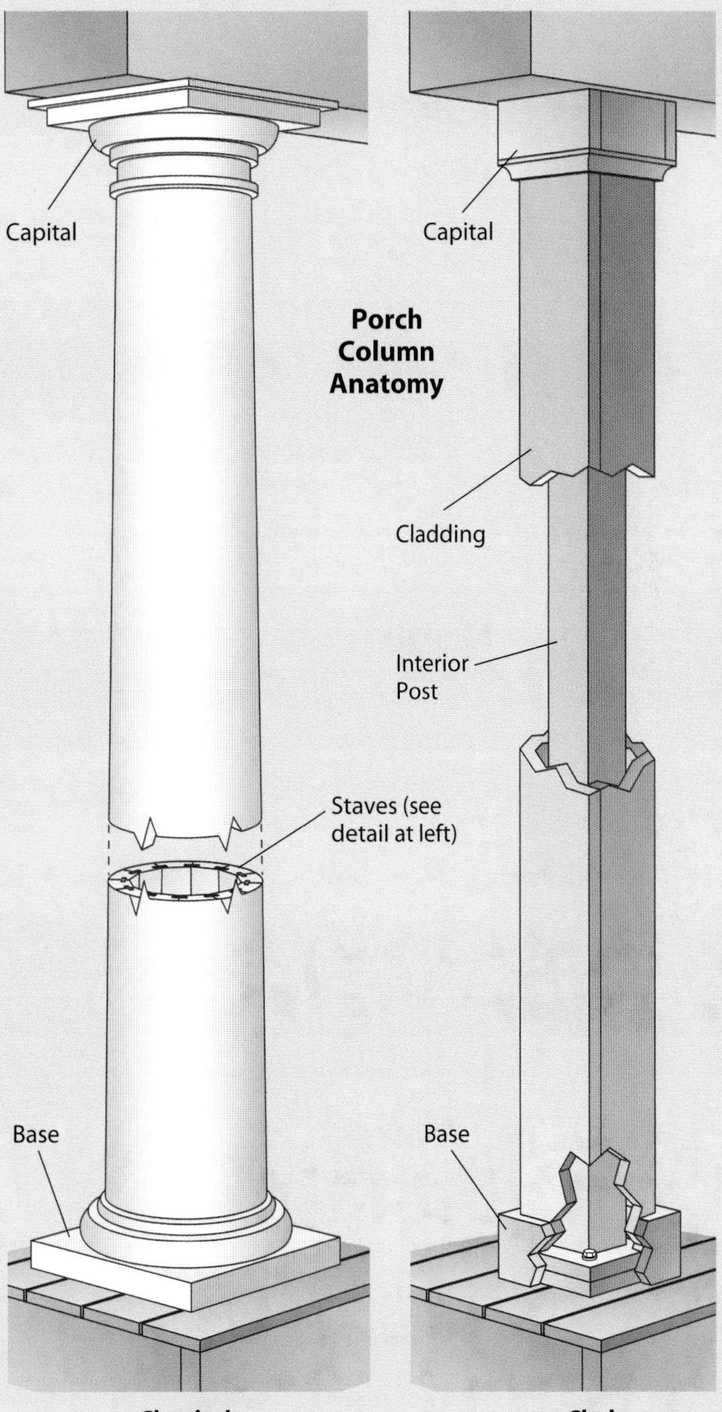

Classical **Clad**

of stone without the expense of custom fabrication or the cost of real stone. Fiberglass and composite columns are widely used. (Early problems with deterioration due to exposure to ultraviolet light seem to have been overcome.) These materials are generally less expensive than cast stone, and they hold paint well. Column capitals and bases made of composite materials are also very

Interesting details add character to columns of any style. At top left, sturdy brackets give a Southwestern look a basic roof structure. Imaginative brackets, bottom left, lend substance and style to a 4x4 porch post. The Ionic capital shone below is complemented by classical dentil and egg-and-dart molding.

Pocket Porches

If one porch isn't enough for you or if you can't find a suitable spot for a full-size porch, consider tucking a pocket porch into a nook or cranny. These little gems (probably more accurately classified as covered balconies) can be found on houses of almost any age or style. Located off a bedroom or study, a pocket porch is a perfect spot for private contemplation or a breath of fresh air.

useful for repairing damaged or decayed columns, as discussed in Chapter 6, "Repair & Maintenance."

RAILINGS

For safety reasons, codes require porch decks that are more than 30 inches above the ground to have railings. Required or not, railings, like posts and columns, can impart considerable character to a porch. Railings come in all shapes, sizes, and styles. You can coordinate them with the overall style of your porch as well as the specific details of posts and columns. Stair railings and deck railings don't have to match, but it's nice if their detailing is somehow complementary.

Ground-level porches, left, require no railings, making for easy access. Masonry piers with wooden columns and peeled railings are a perfect combination for the log house shown below.

During restoration, the deck of this handsome porch was rebuilt; the old porch facade now appears to hover above the ground because it is attached to new hidden deck-support beams and piers.

Bold curves attract the eye to these balusters.

Railings consist of a handrail, balusters, and posts. Porch posts and columns usually double as railing posts, though sometimes separate intermediate or end posts are needed just for railings. (The posts at the ends of a run of railing are often called newel posts.) Handrails can extend over posts, or they can butt into posts that interrupt a run of handrailing.

Materials for railings are the same as for posts and columns, and they have the same advantages and disadvantages. As a carpenter I have to confess my bias toward wooden decks and railings. I like working with wood, and I love the smell of cedar as I shape it into a handrail or baluster. My personal preference also has a practical side. Wood provides the most design options for railings, because

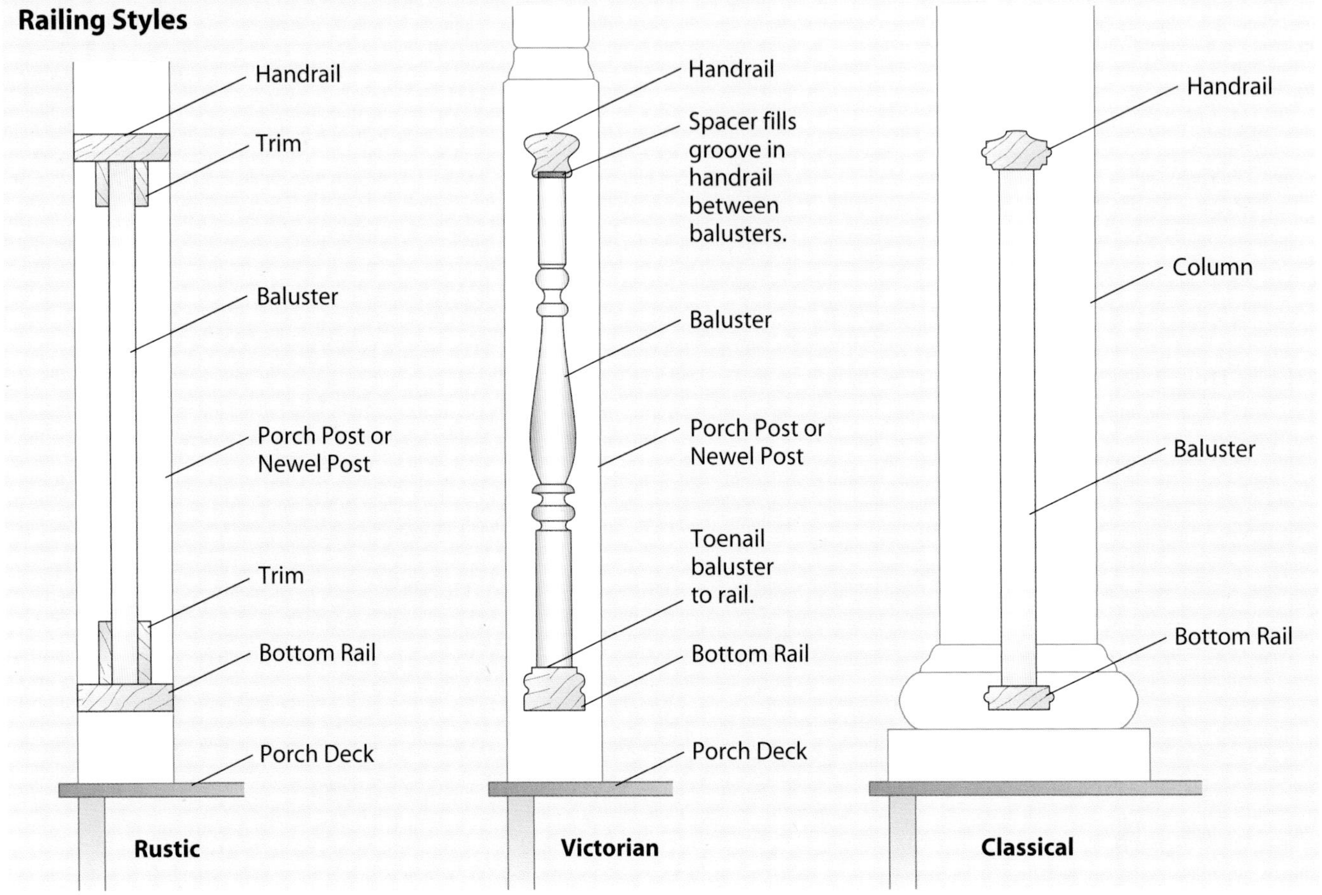

The ornamented railing and skirt on the porch above work together perfectly.

Setting the railing back provides a perch for colorfully planted flower boxes, top right.

Small notches add a subtle decorative touch to a wide-board balustrade, below right.

you or your carpenter can make whatever you want. Non-wood manufactured railings tend to be more expensive than wooden ones, but they don't need painting and are more weather resistant. Most of the companies that manufacture composite decking also offer railing systems.

Half walls of masonry or wood can also serve as railings and are an excellent choice for certain styles of house and porch. Such walls must include *scuppers* at deck level that allow water to drain off the deck. Scuppers can be simple unobtrusive slots or holes along the wall, or they can be part of the decorative scheme. If possible, scuppers should be constructed to channel water far enough out in front of the porch to keep the water from staining the skirting beneath the deck.

Where the railing ties back into the house, you can use a rosette or a half-newel. The rosette is just a flat, solid piece of stock that, once attached to the house, provides a mounting surface for the rail. The half-newel is just what it sounds like; a newel post sawed in half top to bottom. You attach the flat side to the house, and the other side provides flat surfaces at the critical height to accept the top and bottom rails of the balustrade.

Ornate railings provide much more than code-mandated safety. As shown at left and far right opposite, they offer eye-catching interest to porch sitters and passersby alike.

Scuppers drain water from porches with solid half-wall railings, top right.

Railings can be extended to create a safety gate, center right.

This "Union Jack" balustrade is a traditional design, bottom right.

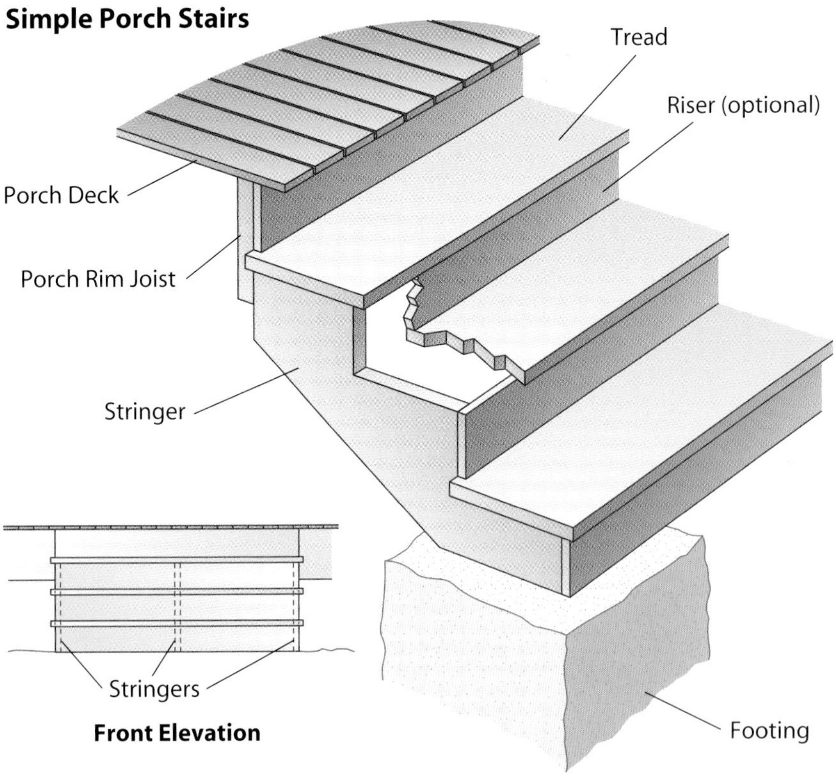

STAIRS

Stairs should be as fancy or as basic as the porches to which they provide access. A rustic set of steps is just right for a log-cabin porch but would ruin the looks of a porch with stately pillars. Whatever their style, porch stairs need to conform to standards in the building codes that specify the height and width of risers and treads and the height of handrails. In cold-winter climates, stairs should rest on footings, as shown in the drawing at left, to prevent freeze-thaw movement. Even if your codes don't require foot-

Stairs are as varied as the porches they serve. The stairs above complement a simple porch. Handrailing in the center of a wide stair, top right, provides support for visitors. The brick stairs, bottom right, are a distinctive addition to this remodeled porch.

Weather-worn timber stairs, with the tool marks from hewing still visible, fit this rustic porch to a tee.

ings, consider installing them; footings help prevent unwanted sloping or sagging over time. Masonry and precast concrete stairs need footings in any climate.

Codes require railings on many stairs. Handrail, balusters, and posts can match those on the porch; some of the composite railing systems sell special stair-railing components. Masonry railings complement porches with masonry walls, piers, or columns. Cast- or wrought-iron stair railings suit a wide range of styles.

The lines of this metal porch roof addition and its connections to the existing house have been carefully thought out to ensure both attractiveness and sound construction.

Anatomy of a Roof

At its simplest, a porch roof consists of rafters covered by sheathing (usually plywood) and shingles or another roofing material, as shown in the drawing. One end of each rafter is fastened to a ledger affixed to the side of the house. The other end rests on a header supported by the porch posts. The connections of the ledger and shingles to the house are critical for the roof's structural integrity and weatherproofing.

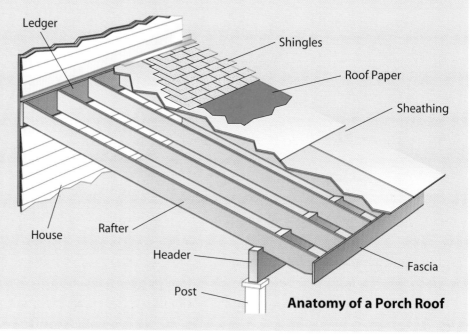

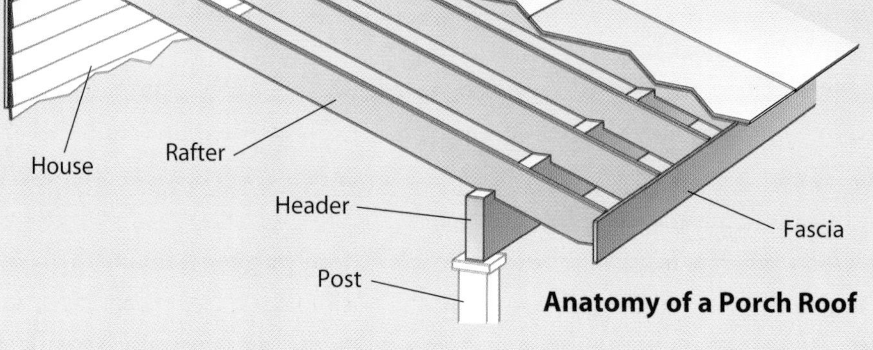

Anatomy of a Porch Roof

Attaching a Porch Roof to the House

When attaching a porch roof to an existing house, it's important that the ledger be attached to the house on the framing rather than over the top of the existing siding. I peel back the clapboards or stucco and nail the ledger through the sub-siding into each stud. For a masonry house, make sure the masonry fasteners are firmly anchored in the brick, stone, or concrete block on the house facade.

After shingling the porch roof, I slip galvanized flashing up under the siding and over the top of the shingles to make the roof watertight. You shouldn't need to caulk anything—if you do, it's a sign that the design or installation of the roof is flawed.

Here, an existing roof is altered to accommodate the gable roof of an addition.

Attaching a New Roof

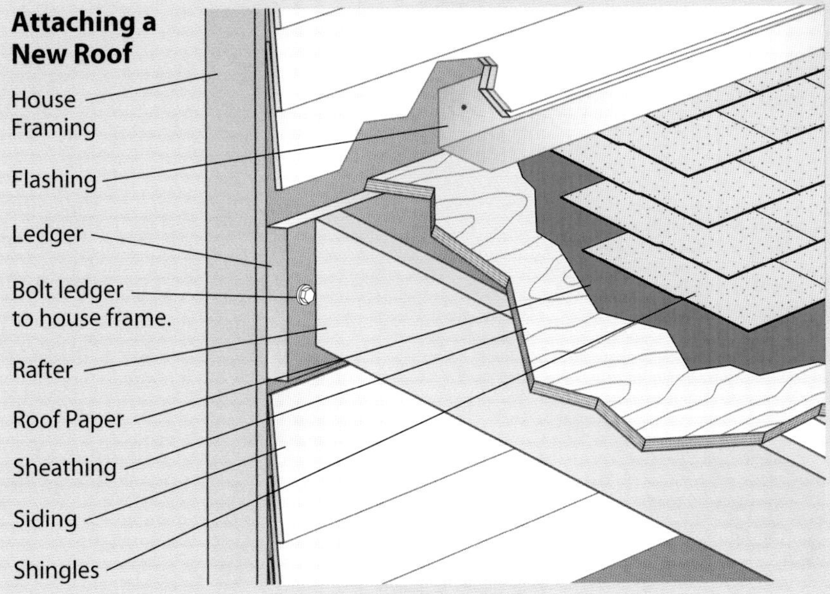

ROOFS

By definition (mine anyway) a porch must have a roof. Offering protection from the rain and shade from the sun, the roof is the reason you sit on the porch rather than out on the lawn. While many of the design details that give character to a porch feature in the posts, piers, columns, and railings, the roof plays an important role in making a porch "fit" the house to which it is attached. If you're adding a new porch, this fit is often accomplished by making the new roof look like the old roof, like it was there all along. This can be done by matching the existing roof pitch, soffits, and fascia and by using a similar roof covering. This isn't difficult or unduly expensive for many houses.

Extending the original roofline over this new porch, above, was made possible, and attractive, by terminating the roof in a curve.

The enclosed gable roof at left creates living space above the porch.

The roof of this house extends over the porch, supported in part by the porch columns, right.

The roof of the porch shown below doubles as a second-story balcony.

Shaped rafters and exposed roof sheathing give the ceiling above a distinctive look.

This clear-finished cedar ceiling, left, and its graceful arch, are a perfect complement to the weathered cedar shake shingles and stonework of the house facade.

If the existing roof is flat, has unusual or expensive tiles or shingles, or has other distinctive features, making a similar porch roof can be costly. If you have such a roof and your budget is tight, a completely different roof style may be just as attractive if its proportions, materials, and details somehow complement the existing roof.

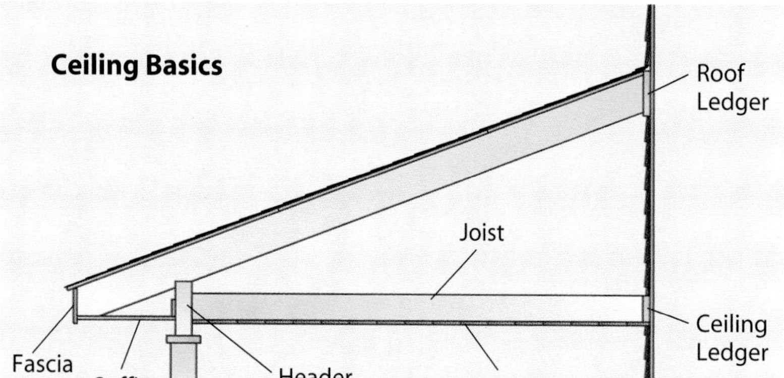

Ceilings

Porch roofs on older homes were often clad on the underside with tongue-and-groove bead-board. Nailed to ceiling joists as shown in the drawing at left, bead-board created a roomlike ceiling, attractive to look at and easy to maintain. Bead-board ceilings aren't inexpensive, but for an elegant look that harkens back to a gentler lifestyle and a decidedly slower pace, they're hard to beat.

Painting the rafters and underside of the roof sheathing with contrasting colors produces a striking effect, top right.

In the dry Southwest, this timber-and-lattice porch roof casts a dappled and cooling shade, bottom right.

If bead-board doesn't fit your pocketbook or your design sense, there are a variety of porch-ceiling alternatives. Simplest is no ceiling at all, just paint or stain the rafters and the underside of the sheathing. Protected from the elements, a ceiling doesn't need a heavy-duty waterproof finish.

To make a porch version of a cathedral ceiling, fix bead-board, solid planks, plywood, or vinyl siding to the rafters. For a flat ceiling, nail the same materials to ceiling joists. I've covered joists or rafters with sheets of rough-sawn cedar plywood and hidden the joints beneath 1×2 cedar strips. Vinyl manufacturers sell a range of soffit materials that provide maintenance-free finishes in several styles. Vinyl is easy and quick to install; it's usually more expensive than plain plywood and less expensive than painted bead-board.

This porch rehab, above and left, required lots of work, but the results are well worth it.

REMODEL & REHAB

As was mentioned in Chapter 1, "Design Possibilities," many houses have existing porches that can be improved or expanded. If you've determined that the basic structural elements are in good condition, you can undertake a wide range of redecorating or remodeling: change siding, trim, and railings; box in old posts or replace them with new; sand and refinish decking; add lights, outlets, a porch swing; add screens or glass.

Built in the 1890s, this house and its porch have been restored. A striking painting scheme highlights details and adds modern-day charm.

Other than finding nasty structural problems once you start work, the main difficulty in remodeling and rehabilitating is matching existing materials. Heed the old cliché: "They don't make 'em like they used to." If you can't find the same decking, siding, brick, or similar materials to make patches or matches, consider replacing rather than patching. Designing your repairs, replacements, and additions with distinctly different materials may prevent your porch from looking as if you tried to match and failed.

If you want a new surface on the wooden decking of an open-air porch, avoid outdoor

Adding Screens

At some times of year in many parts of North America, insects are a serious obstacle to outdoor living. If you can't stand the bugs, an open-air porch or deck may be a battlefield. But a screened-in porch can be a haven. It lets in the breeze but not the bugs.

Screening-in an existing porch is relatively easy. You can simply stretch screen across the existing posts and nail cedar 1x4s to the posts to hold the screen in place. More complicated, but more flexible, is a system of removable screens fitted to a framework inserted between posts. Manufactured screening systems are also available. All of these options require a screen door, of course.

A screened-in porch is just one step removed from a three-season room; before you decide to add screen, check Chapter 4, "Sunrooms & Three-Season Rooms," for extending the seasons by adding glass, too.

These large porch screens offer protection without getting in the way of a beautiful view.

SMART TIP

Power on the Porch. The nicer your porch, the more you'll want to do on it. Whether you're building new or remodeling, it's a good idea to add a couple of outlets along the outside house wall so that you can plug in reading lamps, area fans, radios, and a cord for the rotisserie when you're dining alfresco.

carpeting. Few open-porch decks are sheltered from rain. Wet outdoor carpet takes time to dry, and wood beneath the carpet will take longer to dry. Wood flooring that is wet for long periods will deteriorate over time. Wet wood and carpet are also a conducive environment for mold and mildew.

Porch Furnishings

I've seen everything from overstuffed chairs to modern high-tech furniture on porches. Rocking chairs, candle-lit dining tables, rattan ensembles, sleek steel recliners, and glass-topped occasional tables—it's your porch, you can put whatever you want on it.

You may, however, want to temper your taste with two practical considerations, durability and portability. Durability because the furniture will be used outside. And portability because you may want to take it inside when you're not using it.

If you like wooden furniture, note that outdoor furniture made of naturally rot-resistant woods such as redwood, cedar, white oak, and teak needs no finish and, therefore, less maintenance. Over the years all these woods will weather to an attractive silver gray with exposure to the elements. In

A screened porch, above, is ideal for evening entertainments free of uninvited insect guests. A coat of black paint is an unusual but effective touch on this durable wicker porch furniture, below.

Porch Fans

For those lazy, hot summer days when nary a breath of wind stirs the soul or the air on the porch, you might consider a ceiling-mounted porch fan. Several manufacturers offer models built to endure the temperature extremes and humidity in the outdoor environment of a porch.

general, wooden indoor furniture will fall apart faster outdoors than it would indoors. The joints, glues, and finishes are not designed for exposure to weather; even high humidity will damage them.

Metal furniture, from light-weight twisted wire to ornate cast iron, is also popular for porches. Painted versions are less expensive, but powder coating, which is a baked-on finish, is more durable. Aluminum, of course, requires no weather protection. Add a glass-top table and a couple of end tables for the easy chair, and you're ready to relax and enjoy the outdoors.

A traditional porch swing, left, offers a comfortable seat and a whisper of a breeze to cool you on a hot day. If you don't have room for a swing, a rocker or two, above, will substitute nicely. Casual contemporary furnishings combine easily with classic wicker on the porch below.

Landscaping

Plants help fulfill the happy marriage between the indoors and the outdoors embodied in a porch. Plantings have a practical side. Trees and shrubs can provide shade and screen wind; if they're deciduous, leaf drop allows the sun to warm the porch into the autumn.

Plants mask the opening beneath this raised porch with an eye-catching display of flowers and foliage.

A climbing rose on a trellis makes an ideal privacy screen and focal point for this porch.

Installed for purely ornamental reasons, plants are no less valuable to your enjoyment of a porch. Today, foundation plantings (landscaping up next to the base of a porch or house) are more adventurous and interesting than the tidy row of clipped evergreens common for too many years. Handsome foliage and colorful flowers of small trees, shrubs, and perennials can be appreciated from porch and sidewalk. Vines climbing up railings, posts, and columns bring the sights and fragrances closer to porch sitters. Hanging baskets, planting boxes lining a railing, or plant-filled terra-cotta pots provide ample space for a seasonal display of annuals. ■

Pavers and plantings extend the gathering space of the porch above.

CHAPTER 4

Sunrooms & Three-Season Rooms

At its simplest, a three-season room or sunroom is a porch modified to keep the weather out. A three-season room protects you from wind, rain, and snow, but it isn't heated or cooled. A sunroom not only keeps the elements out, it offers a heated and cooled environment like any other room in your house. If you're looking for a protected spot to get some fresh air and you don't mind what temperature that air is, consider a three-season room. If you're a sun lover who'd rather not brave freezing cold or oppressive heat to bask in the sunlight, think about a sunroom. In this chapter we'll look at what goes into creating each of these rooms.

ROOM OPTIONS

You can convert an existing porch to a three-season room by installing glass and screen panels and a storm door between posts or columns. Or you can build a new three-season addition with floor-to-ceiling window-and-screen panels.

Because it is uninsulated and unheated, a three-season room won't get much winter use in cold climates. But on those late fall or early spring days when a porch would be uncomfortably chilly, a three-season room can warm up nicely as radiant heat from the sun is captured in the enclosed space. Where winters are warm, the off season may be the summer, when the uninsulated, unairconditioned space may get too toasty.

Sunrooms are by definition habitable in all seasons, though the demands of insulation, heating, and cooling make them more expensive than three-season rooms. They may be conversions of porches, patios, or decks. They can be custom-made from the ground up. Or they can be manufactured and installed in a matter of days.

Many sunrooms are highly finished and indistinguishable in style, detail, and furnish-

This manufactured addition could be either a three-season room or a sunroom, depending on the type of glass and insulation chosen.

ings from other rooms in the house. Or they may have a distinctive style all their own.

Whether they are conversions, custom built, or factory made, three-season rooms and sunrooms have many similarities. Their basic structures are often the same. Replace single-pane glass with insulated glass and add insulation to the walls, floors, and roof, and add a source of heating and cooling, and a three-season room becomes a sunroom.

Because of the similarities between three-season rooms and sunrooms, I'll discuss both in this chapter, noting distinctions as I go.

Porch Conversions

Many open-air porches can be converted to three-season rooms. How easily this can be done depends a great deal on how ornate the porch is. It's relatively simple to install window and screen units and a door on a porch

Framing a Porch for Windows

If an opening on a porch is already rectangular and is plumb and level, you can size a custom-built window and frame to fit in that opening, attached to the posts, deck or railing, and top beam. Or you can frame new openings to fit standard-size manufactured windows or custom windows of a size you desire. Windows for porch conversions are often housed in wood frames, because a carpenter can often make them on site. You can also have aluminum frames custom-built with individual windows and screens made to fit.

If porch openings are irregularly shaped, it's usually more cost-effective to modify the openings than to build oddly shaped windows. This is especially true for windows with moving parts such as sashes or louvers. Porches with round or molded columns, sloped floors, or elaborate brackets can be framed to accept rectilinear windows, as shown in the drawings. Porch decks usually slope away from the house. Openings for windows added along the slope are best framed to create a level bottom because rectilinear windows are much cheaper than trapezoidal ones. Note also that glass that rests less than 18 inches above the deck is required by code to be tempered, which will increase the cost. You can frame the opening higher to accommodate standard glass.

Simple Framing for Porch Windows

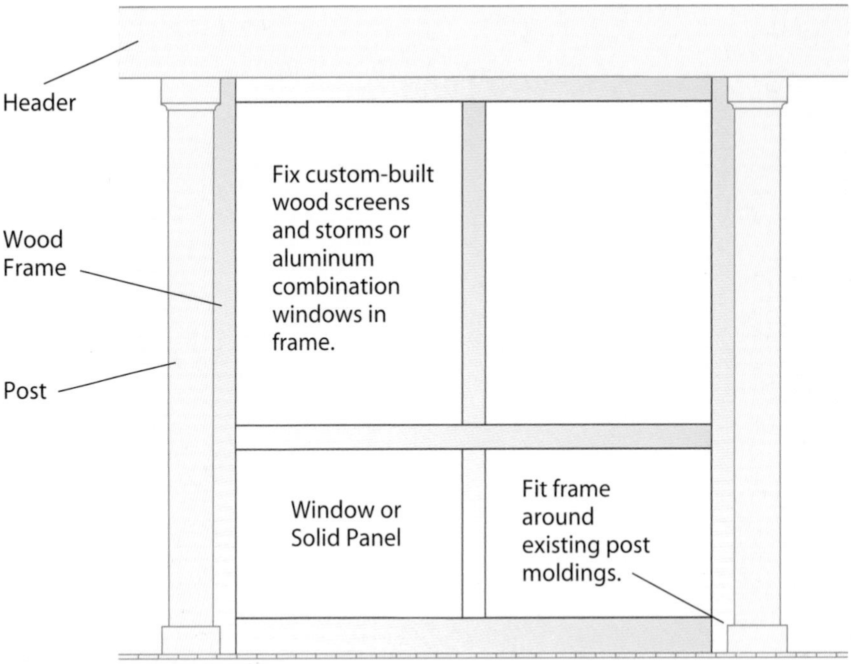
Header
Wood Frame
Post
Fix custom-built wood screens and storms or aluminum combination windows in frame.
Window or Solid Panel
Fit frame around existing post moldings.

Scribed Framing for Porch Windows

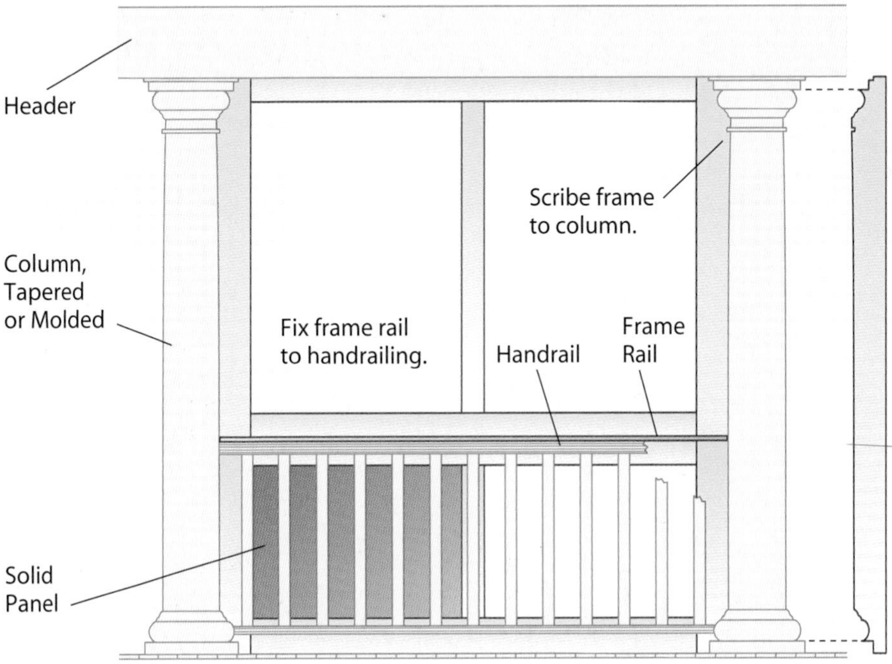
Header
Column, Tapered or Molded
Solid Panel
Scribe frame to column.
Fix frame rail to handrailing.
Handrail
Frame Rail

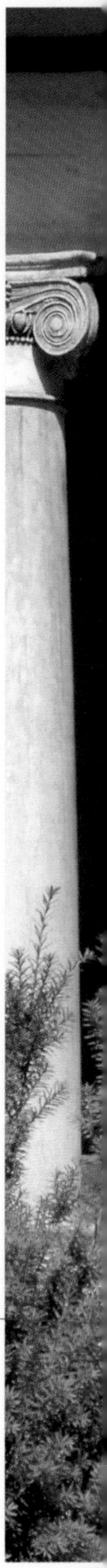

A window frame has been carefully scribed to the Ionic capital and base and the gentle curve of the column shaft in the conversion shown below.

that has rectilinear posts and simple railings. Adding windows and a door to a porch that has tapered or heavily molded columns, elaborate brackets, and complex or curved railings requires more thought, more construction skills, and usually more money. (See "Framing a Porch for Windows," left.)

A manufactured room was cleverly adapted to convert this porch to a three-season room.

Straight columns are relatively easy to fill in to enclose a porch, far left. Turned columns and a railing, at left, make enclosing a porch a more complicated project.

Embedded in the wall, the original porch columns are a striking feature of this converted sunroom, opposite.

Traditional wooden storm windows and screens enclose this three-season porch conversion.

Floor-to-ceiling screens allow ample light and air into this three-season room. Note the careful scribing around the ceiling joists.

Door, window, and screen units are often much the same for simple and complicated installations alike. (Specifics about windows and doors are covered later in the chapter.) The extra cost and installation finesse comes from figuring out how to fill in between rectangular door, window, and screen units and the existing curved and filigreed porch columns and railings.

Converting a porch to a sunroom is a bit more difficult and expensive. Insulated windows and doors are costlier than those with single-pane glass. Insulating an existing porch floor and roof isn't necessarily expensive or difficult, but it may not be terribly effective, either. Nevertheless, charming sunrooms have been made from porches.

Before you consider how to convert an existing porch, make sure it is structurally sound. Check for good footings and foundations; no rotting or deteriorating posts, joists, floor boards, or roof members; and no leaning or tilting. If it's going to cost a lot of money to fix the structure before you convert the space, you should probably tear off the existing porch and build from scratch.

Converting a Deck

A deck is often an ideal site for a three-season room or sunroom addition. Decks are usually located where sun, shade, and wind conditions on your property are optimal. They are usually adjacent to a room in the house that is desirable for connection to a three-season room or sunroom. They may already have a door or sliding door suitable for access to the new room. And they can provide, at the least, a ready-made floor or subfloor.

Before you convert a deck, you'll need to check its footings to see if they are large enough to carry the additional load of walls

Converting a Deck

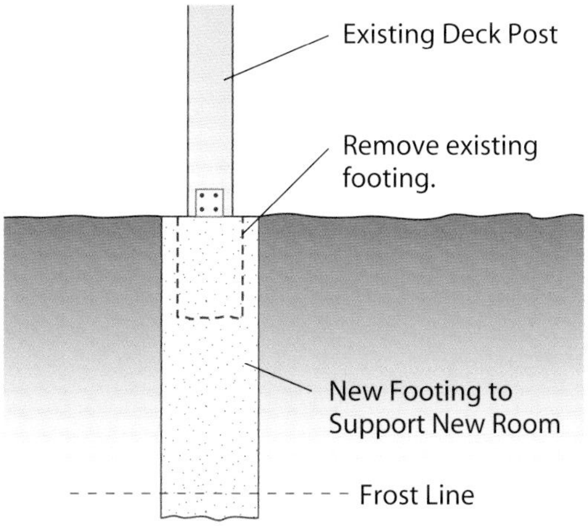

The manufactured vinyl sunroom below was built on top of an existing deck, shown above. Note the addition of a central post to support the extra weight.

A second-story deck offers the possibility of adding a sunroom above and a three-season room below, as shown above.

and roof. A contractor or codes department can help you with the calculations. If the footings are insufficient, you may be able to enlarge them with additional concrete. Or you may need to build temporary supports, tear out the existing footings, and re-pour.

The sunroom shown below is a handsome replacement for a simple covered patio.

Patio Conversions

Because most patios are just a slab of concrete lying on the ground, you'll need to add footings to support the room's structure. The most cost-effective way to do this is to trench footings around the outside of the slab and erect the walls on those footings, with the slab "floating" inside the footings. If the patio is larger than the room you want to add, you can cut through the concrete and pour trench footings for the walls. This process can cost more than demolishing the patio and building from scratch, so do a thorough evaluation before undertaking it.

Most patios slope away from the house for drainage. The typical slope of ¼ inch per foot isn't very noticeable in use and can be fine for the floor of a simple three-season room. For a more finished three-season room or sunroom, you'll probably want a level floor. You can top-coat an existing slab with a special coating made for leveling. Several brands are available. Some require flooring (or an additional treatment if you want exposed concrete) to protect the surface coating from wear.

Converting a Patio

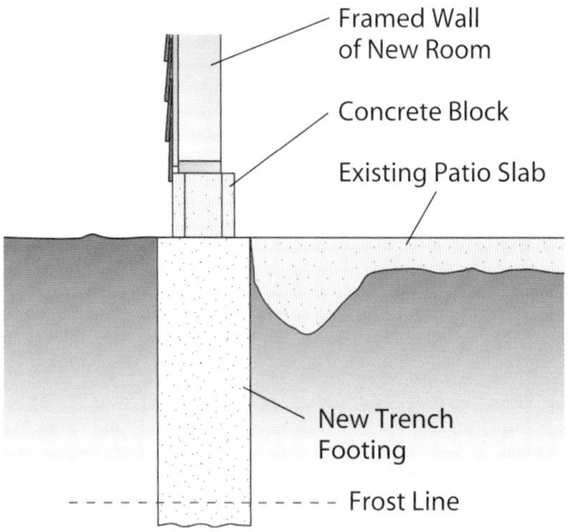

An existing patio was the starting point for this manufactured room.

Custom-built three-season rooms or sunrooms can incorporate any material, construction technique, and style to provide exactly what you want.

THREE-SEASON & SUNROOM ADDITIONS

If you want a three-season room or sunroom but don't have a porch, deck, or patio to convert, you'll need to add a new structure on to your house. There are two construction options: a custom-designed and custom-built addition or a manufactured room. The custom approach is usually the more expensive, but it allows more flexibility in design and materials. Manufactured rooms can be installed more quickly, and they can take advantage of some processes and materials unavailable to most local contractors. Because the rooms are manufactured in factories, the quality can be closely monitored.

A manufactured room can be as striking as one that has been custom built, as the sunroom shown on this page proves. Note the use of the existing brick facade as an interior wall.

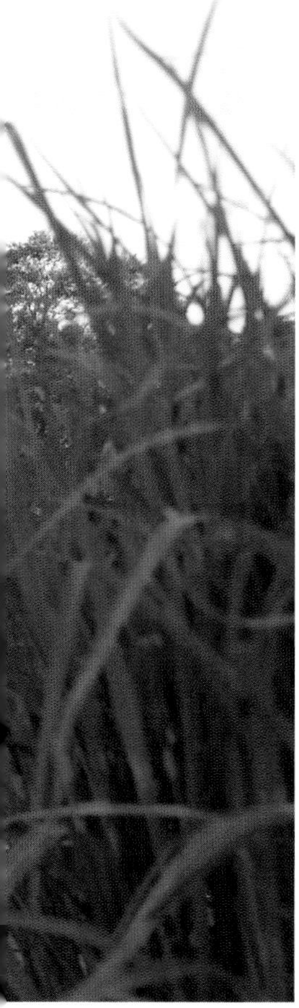

As discussed in Chapter 1, "Design Possibilities," the choice of where to put a three-season room or sunroom addition depends largely on the inside layout of your house and the new room's orientation to the sun. You'll need convenient access to the room from inside and outside. You may be able to use an existing door, but more likely you'll have to convert a window or punch a hole in an exterior wall to accommodate a door or sliding doors. You can leave everything else in the inside and outside of the house—windows,

This manufactured sunroom addition and its surrounding water-garden landscaping is beautiful inside and outside, as is shown on these pages.

siding, trim, and so on—as they are, or you may choose to remove or replace them, depending on your desires and budget.

CUSTOM-BUILT ROOMS

Custom building can give you a three-season room or sunroom that fits seamlessly with the rest of your house, creating an addition that doesn't look like an addition. This is also the approach if yours is a vision of something completely different—allowing free reign to your imagination (constrained, of course, by cost and codes). Many styles can be built cost-effectively with conventional construction, shown in the drawings on this page and discussed on the following pages.

Three-Season Room Construction

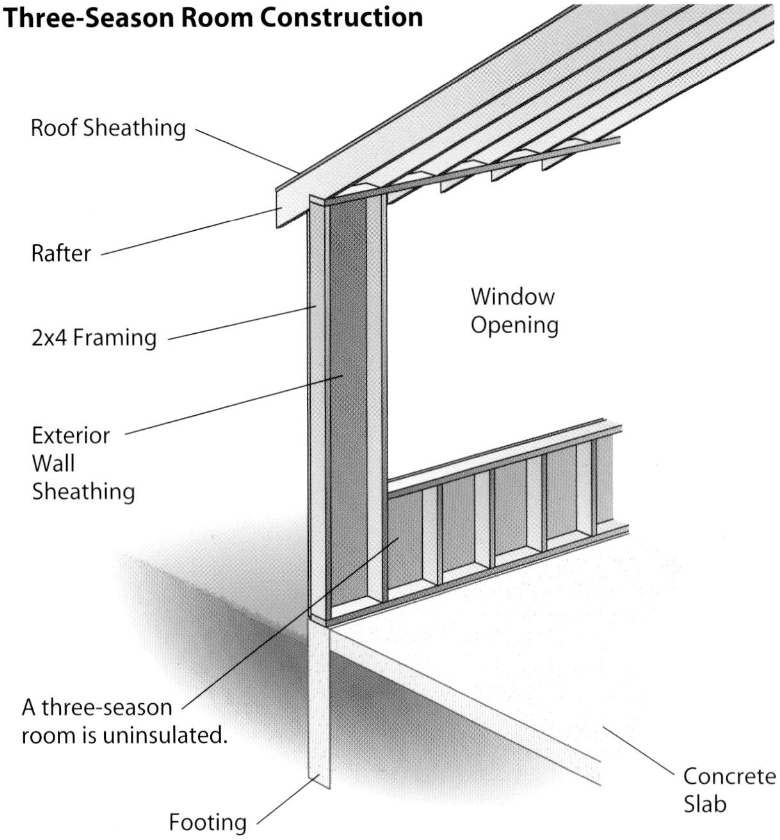

Sunroom Construction

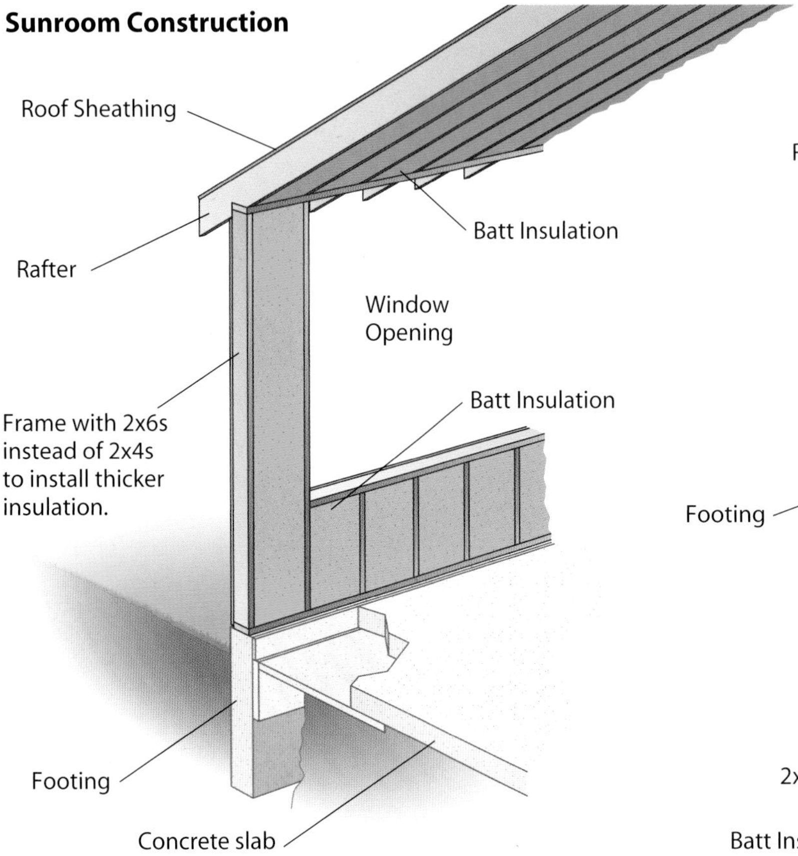

Roof Detail

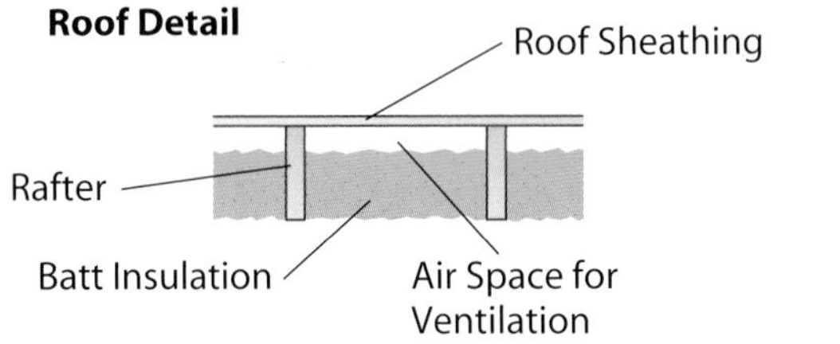

Floor Detail

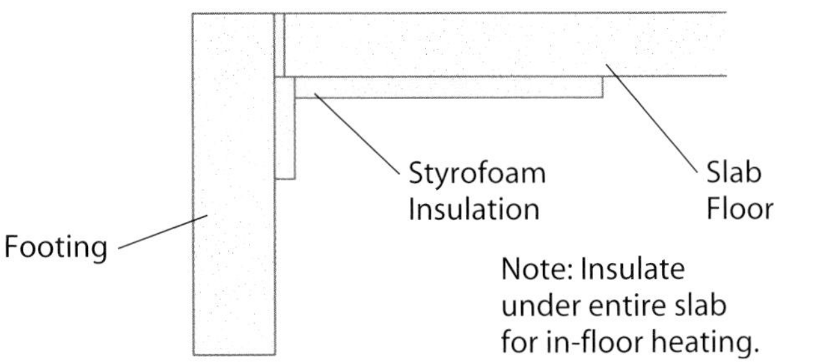

Wall Detail

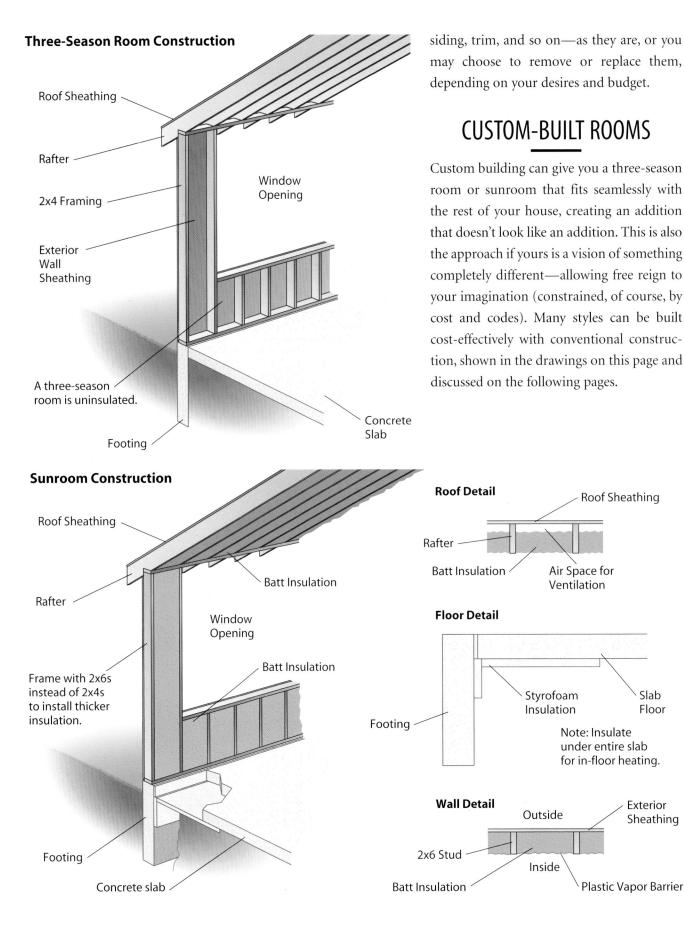

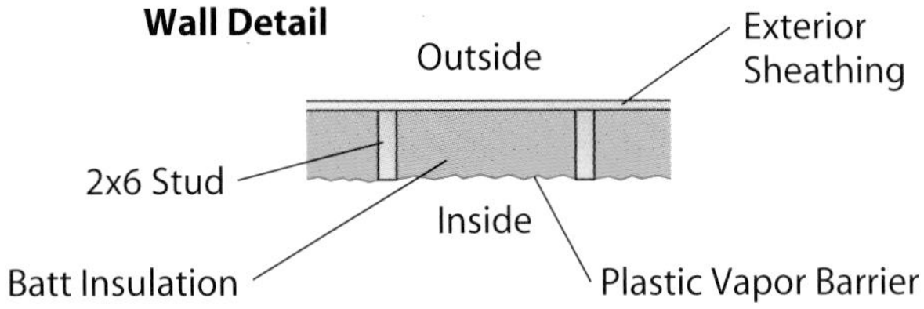

Old-fashioned metal casement windows provide this three-season room with lots of light and a distinctive look.

Support Your Floor

Tongue-and-groove oriented strand board (OSB) subflooring, glued and nailed or glued and screwed to the joists, makes a good base for carpet in a three-season room or sunroom. But it's a little rough for linoleum or vinyl tiles. The joints between the sheets of OSB tend to pucker and telegraph through these surfaces. For linoleum and tile, I fix sheets of 1/4-inch or 3/8-inch underlayment plywood on top of the OSB. Underlayment plywood has no voids in internal plys, so it provides a solid backing for linoleum. (The plywood must be installed with some spacing at the joints so it won't pucker with expansion.) I also install 3/8-inch underlayment plywood when converting a deck to a sun- or three-season room. The plywood bridges the small gaps between deck boards and provides a durable backing for either carpet or linoleum.

Ceramic tile makes a handsome, durable floor, but it requires a very rigid substrate to prevent the grout in the joints from loosening or, worse, the tiles from cracking over time. The best tile substrate, of course, is a concrete slab. This is a reasonable option if you're converting an existing patio; it's an expensive option if you have to pour the slab on top of floor joists. Cement board, a more rigid material than underlayment plywood, is often applied over OSB as a tile substrate. But movement in the floor joists can still loosen grout in the tile joints. Conventionally framed floors move, even those covered with cement board. It's unavoidable. And the larger the span, the more the floor moves. Deeper or more closely spaced joists may help, but I think a better solution is a stressed-skin panel floor. (See "Stressed-Skin Panels" on page 158). Stressed-skin panels are more rigid than conventional construction, especially if you add an additional beam or two to decrease the distance the panels span.

Supporting Carpet, Vinyl Tile, Linoleum

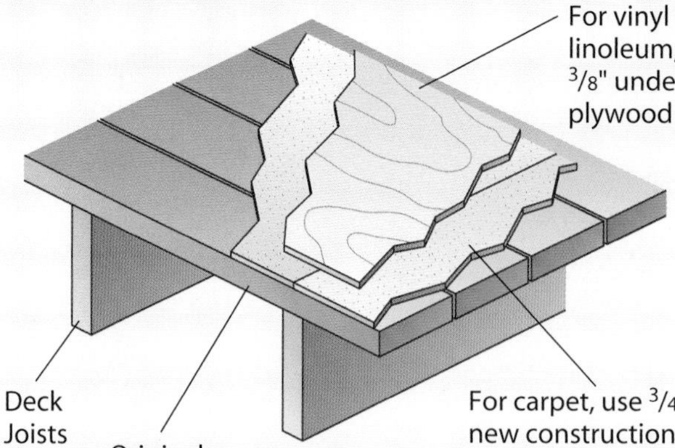

Ceramic Tile on Stressed-Skin Panel

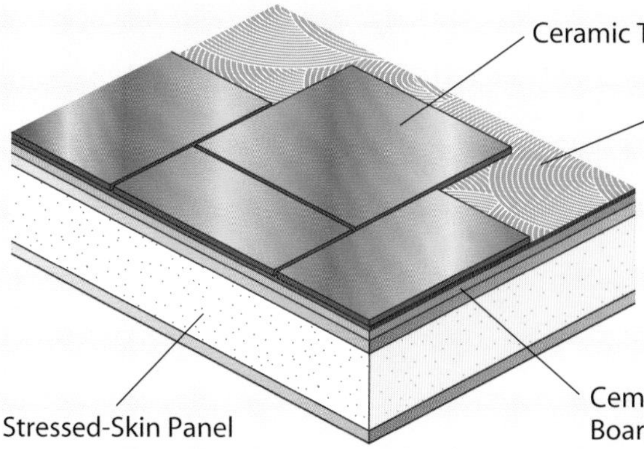

Ceramic Tile on Raised Slab

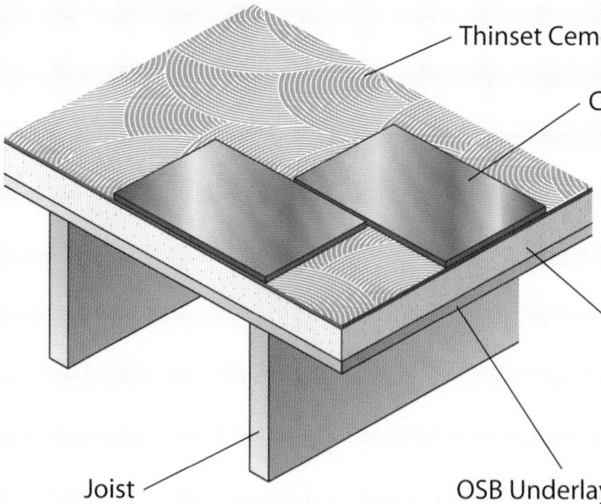

Floors

Like any other addition to your house, a three-season room or sunroom must have code-compliant footings, foundations, and attachments to the existing structure. Concrete footings and a slab can provide this support, as can posts, piers, or walls of wood or masonry resting on in-ground footings.

If the floor joists and floor of the room are 18 inches or more above the ground, they do not need to be chemically treated to retard deterioration. So, in general, you can conventionally frame the deck with SPF (spruce, pine, fir) lumber and OSB (oriented strand board) subflooring. Because the floor is protected from weather, the range of materials for its finished surface is greater than that for an open-air porch. Carpet, linoleum, wood (conventional or snap-together laminates), or ceramic tile are possibilities. Depending on your choice, however, you may need to provide additional underlayment or beef-up the joists, as discussed in "Support Your Floor," opposite.

A painted wood floor adds a little zip to this sunroom.

Insulating a Floor

Heat rises, so an insulated floor isn't going to save a lot of warm air, which will migrate out through the walls, windows, and roof. But a warm floor is more comfortable than a cold one, so I recommend insulating it. On a porch or deck conversion, it's usually easiest to install fiberglass batt insulation under the floor between the joists, nailing on a plywood cover to contain the insulation. (See the drawing at right.)

If you're building from scratch and using a framed floor, you can increase the thickness of the batts (and therefore their insulating quality) by using deeper floor joists than are required to carry the load. Another option is

Raised Floor

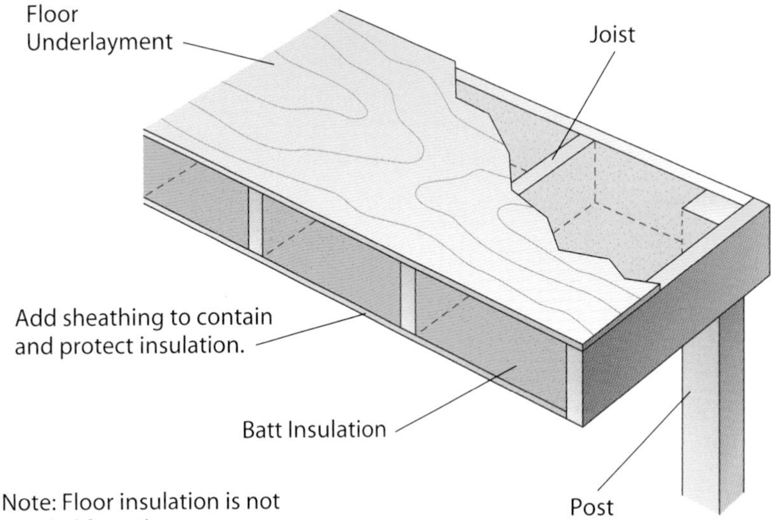

Note: Floor insulation is not needed for a three-season room.

Slate flooring, above, and ceramic tiles, opposite, are excellent sunroom surfaces. They're durable and attractive, and they're also a passive solar heat source.

to enclose and insulate the crawl space beneath the sunroom floor. It used to be common practice to vent a crawl space and insulate the floor above. I've always thought this a difficult and poor practice. The U.S. Department of Energy now agrees with me, recommending that you seal the crawl space and insulate the inside surfaces of its walls. (They caution that this practice may still be contrary to local codes.) It's important to cover the ground in the crawl space to slow the evaporation and condensation of ground moisture. I generally use 6-mil plastic and cover it with pea gravel to protect it and hold it in place.

If you're pouring a concrete floor, make sure the footings and slab are insulated, as shown in "Sunroom Construction," page 132. It's also important to make a "thermal break" between the footings and the slab. Concrete is a poor insulator; heat passes right through it, so it cools down very fast. If the concrete footings on the outside of the room are freezing, the concrete floor will also be freezing unless there is a barrier between the two, as the drawing shows.

Both slab and framed floors can be made with in-floor heating (an electrical or a fluid-based system). If you choose this option, ask your contractor about necessary insulation.

Wreathed in vines and window boxes on the outside, opposite, the walls of this cozy room are paneled with bead-board on the inside, above.

Walls

Because you want lots of sun in a sunroom, the wall structure must accommodate a lot of windows. Conventional stud walls with 2×4s spaced on 16-inch or 24-inch centers can do this. The simplest wall system for lots of glass is a post-and-beam frame built on the subfloor. Post-and-beam walls consist of large posts (4×4s or 6×6s) spaced 3 feet or more apart and connected by horizontal beams. This construction style, often called timber frame, is shown at right.

If you don't want glass everywhere, it's possible to fill between posts with conventional framing. If you want to leave the posts

Post-and-Beam Walls

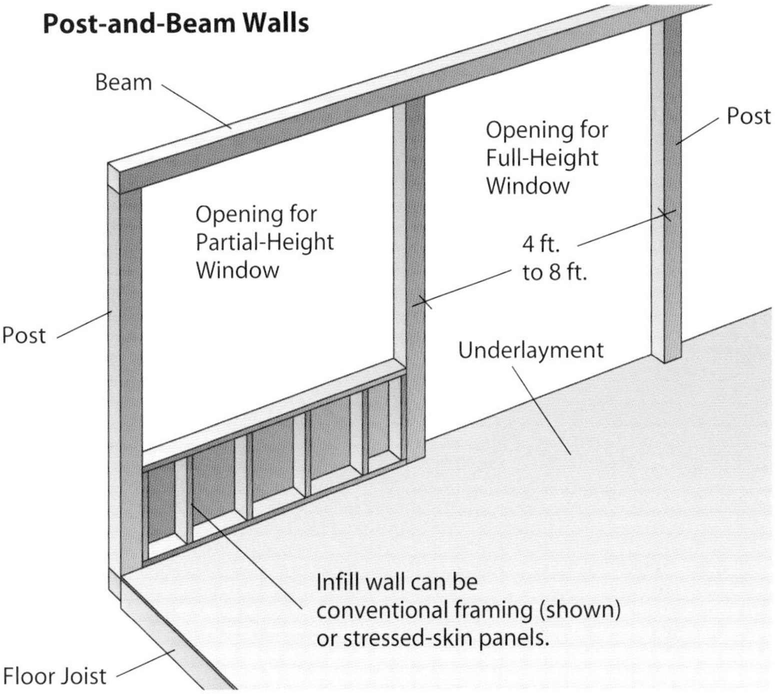

Double doors in traditional stud framing form the walls in this handsome sunroom.

exposed for decorative reasons on the outside, inside, or both, you can fill the spaces between posts with stucco, wood, or masonry. Making these fill-ins watertight requires an experienced installer.

A timber-frame addition allows for a lot of glass, but such structures are often difficult to blend in with the existing house. Conventional 2×4 framing is easier to tie into existing exterior siding or masonry, and to match the trim style on doors, windows, eaves, and so on. The interior can also be finished like the other rooms in your house, if you wish.

SMART TIP

Wired Up. Though a three-season room is, by definition, neither heated nor cooled, there's no reason it can't accommodate other modern conveniences—computers, TVs, stereos, and other electrical devices we've come to expect or depend on in our homes. If you want the wires and cables to disappear in the walls or under the floor, make sure they're installed during construction, not after.

This custom-built sunroom incorporates metal columns purchased at a local home store and adapted to suit the design.

Insulating Walls

Sunroom walls are mostly glass, but where possible, you should insulate around the windows, the framed area above and below the windows, and in the corners.

Fiberglass insulation works by maintaining a certain "loft" or fullness. If it's packed in too tight, it loses its effectiveness; it can also deflect the jamb of a window or door and make it hard to open or close. Using too much expansive foam insulation can also cause the same deflection problem.

If you're doing the insulation yourself, I recommend using unfaced, friction-fit fiberglass batt insulation in the walls, as shown on page 132. It's inexpensive and easy to install. Just tuck the batts between the wall studs, and cut it snugly around outlets and wiring. Clear 4-mil plastic sheeting stapled to the studs makes a better vapor barrier than the paper on paper-backed fiberglass insulation.

Vapor barriers are the cause of much confusion among home owners (and too many professionals). In cold climates, a vapor barrier prevents the migration into the insulation of warm, moist air from inside the room. Without the barrier, this air would meet colder, outside air inside the wall. The

Walls: Inside Surface

Conditions, particularly humidity, inside three-season rooms and sunrooms often differ enough to require different wall treatments.

Three-season Rooms

I discourage clients from using drywall on the interior wall and ceiling surfaces in the three-season rooms I build. In Nebraska, where I live, summertime humidity is high, and the open conditions in the room invite condensation, which leads to mildew or worse on drywall. (Before the advent of central air conditioning, most interior wall surfaces were plastered rather than drywalled; plaster is much less susceptible to damage from humidity.)

Where humidity is low year-round, drywall may be trouble-free. No matter where you live, if you can't depend on the many windows in a three-season room being shut every time it rains, you should consider an interior wall treatment less likely to turn mushy when it gets wet.

In the semi-exterior conditions of a three-season interior, I prefer wood or weather-resistant plywood, OSB, or laminate paneling for wall coverings and trim. Tongue-and-groove pine bead-board looks as terrific in a three-season room as on a porch, whether painted, stained, or clear-finished. Cedar, redwood, and other naturally weather-resistant woods are equally effective.

Sunrooms

Because sunrooms are heated and cooled, any interior wall surface you'd use elsewhere in your house is acceptable. Drywall, paneling, masonry, and wallpaper are all options. If you choose wallpaper, remember that sunlight fades some colors, and there will be a lot of sunlight.

Clapboard and board-and-batten walls fit well in simple rustic rooms or in more elegant settings, as shown in the sunrooms above and at right.

The muted but varied tones of a cut-stone wall add interest to this sunroom.

Options for large sunroom windows include fixed, opposite top and bottom, and sliding, above. Stressed-skin panels form the solid areas of wall in the opposite top photo.

cold air condenses the moisture in the warm air and you end up with wet insulation, which loses its insulation value and is an ideal site for mold and mildew.

Where the climate is warm and humid year-round, some builders install a vapor barrier on the outside of an exterior wall. In such a climate, the inside of the room is kept cool and dry relative to the outside heat and humidity. Hence, the condensation risk is from moisture trying to migrate into the room from the outside. I'm a little skeptical that the air conditioning will drop the temperature inside the wall enough to trigger condensation, but if you live in such a climate, it's probably prudent to check with your builder or codes department about where to put the vapor barrier.

WINDOWS

Windows are the most important feature of sunrooms and three-season rooms. They let in light and keep out weather. The more window area you have the more light you let in and the greater the view you can enjoy.

Unfortunately, windows in general, and glass in particular, are poor insulators. Heat and cold move through them easily. In terms of thermal resistance, a window functions

SMART TIP

Smart Windows. For those interested in the cutting edge of high-tech, it's possible to buy "super windows" with a center-of-glass R-value of 8 or 9. But when edge and frame are factored in, the overall R-value is still only about 4 or 5. On the horizon are "smart windows," both active and passive, that will vary their ability to transmit both heat and light, depending on temperature and time of day.

With a minimal but sturdy aluminum framework, the walls in the sunroom shown above left are almost entirely glass.

Double-hung windows, above right, have separate upper and lower sashes, both of which slide open.

more like a hole in a wall than like a part of the wall. That said, windows have come a long way from the single-pane, double-hung windows in many older homes, where when the wind blew, the curtains moved.

Three-Season Windows

For unheated, uncooled three-season rooms, insulation is not a concern. Single-pane glass is much cheaper than modern double-pane insulated glass and it comes in a variety of window styles. Combination storm windows and screens are inexpensive and adaptable. Fit them into simple wooden frames between porch posts and you're well on your way to converting an existing porch to a new three-season room. Because of their popularity for weatherproofing old (and new) houses, combination storm windows are widely available in most towns through dealers or fabricators. Combination storm windows usually have aluminum frames and can be custom-made to any size.

The drawback of combination storms, whether they are single hung, double hung, or slide from side to side, is that they allow air through only half the opening. To provide more airflow, you can buy casement windows, which crank open on hinges, like a door. Some manufacturers also offer double-

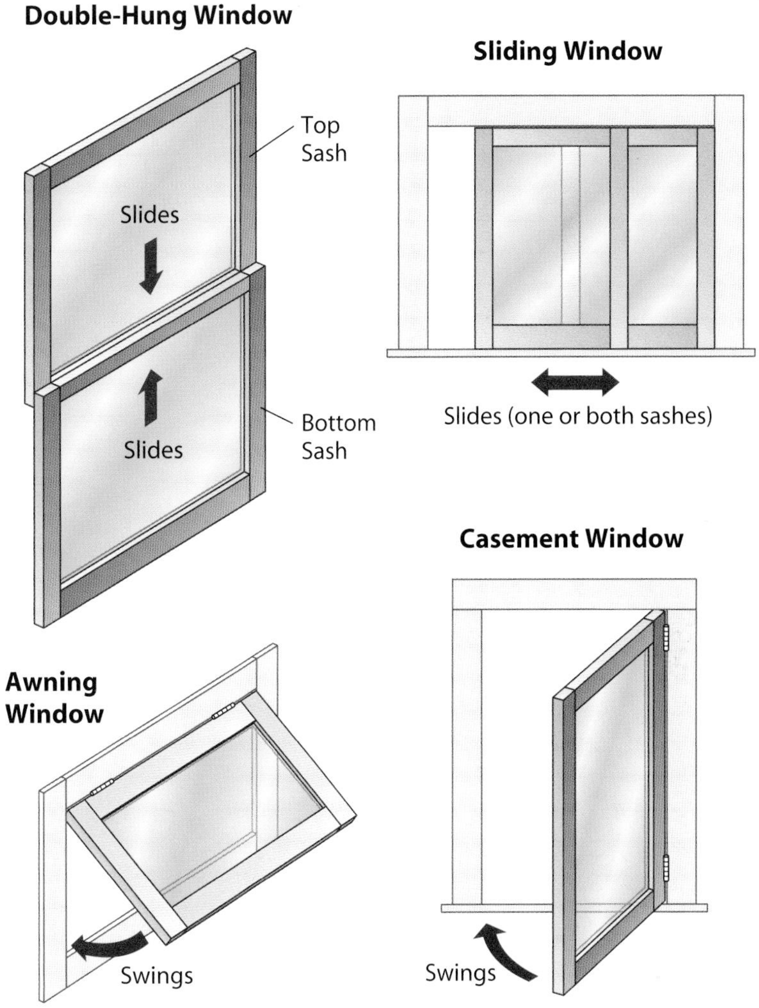

hung windows in which both sashes can be removed, so in nice weather you can have a full-screen porch, though you'll need a place to store all those sashes.

Instead of housing the windows in wood frames, you can have aluminum frames custom built with individual windows and screens made to fit. Though simpler than combination storms and capable of providing more airflow, this system requires that you remove the glass panels—and store them—when you want more fresh air.

If you'd like your three-season room windows to resemble those in the rest of your house, many manufacturers offer stock or custom-built sash or casement windows in a range of styles. These windows can be made of wood, wood clad in vinyl or aluminum, or of aluminum, vinyl, or fiberglass. Unfortunately, buying real windows rather than combination storms can be pricey. With the extra cost of windows, you might consider building a sunroom.

Windows for Sunrooms

You can install the same kind of uninsulated windows in a sunroom as in a three-season room. But with so much wall surface given to windows, your heating and cooling bills will be astronomical. Double-pane insulated

The ABCs of Insulated Windows

Modern insulated windows include features to counter each of the three primary ways that windows transfer heat: Non-solar, solar, and airflow.

Non-solar heat transfer involves the heating or cooling of the window materials themselves (glass, wood, metal). Radiant heat from the sun and heat from the surrounding air warm the window glass and frame, which in turn transfer this heat to the air inside the room. Non-solar heat transfer is measured and expressed as the U-value, a less widely known term than R-value, used to rate fiberglass and other insulators. R-value is a measure of a material's resistance to heat transfer. U-value is a measure of a material's facilitation of heat transfer. If you're trying to prevent the transfer of heat, you want materials with high R-values and low U-values. For a variety of reasons, U-values rather than R-values provide a better indication of window performance, so that's the rating provided by window manufacturers.

Glass is a poor insulator, but nonmoving air is a good insulator, and a vacuum is even better. Hence the development of double-paned windows, where two sheets of glass are separated by an air space or by a vacuum, which impedes the transfer of heat from one pane to the other. Some gases insulate better than ordinary air, so in many double-pane windows, the space between the panes is filled with argon, krypton, sulfur hexafluoride, or carbon dioxide.

Double-pane windows are a big improvement over single-pane regarding the transfer of heat. But it is worth noting that they're still just windows. An argon-filled double-pane window has an R-value of about 3. An R-value of about 20 is a minimum standard for an insulated wall.

Solar heat gain is how the sun warms the earth. Space is a vacuum, so there's no medium, such as air or metal, to transfer the heat to the earth. The light itself (solar radiation) warms the object on which it falls. Thus a cat on a cold porch warms itself by lazing in a pool of sunlight.

Glass offers little protection against heat gain by solar radiation. That's a good thing in the dead of a cold winter, but not so desirable in a hot summer. Window manufacturers employ two methods to reduce solar heat gain. Low-emissivity (Low-E) coating is a microscopically thin, virtually invisible metal or metal oxide film applied to the inside surfaces of double-pane glass. Or, manufacturers may install a thin plastic film between the glass surfaces. These films reflect solar radiation in such a way that a room is cooler when outside temperatures are hot and warmer when outside temperatures are cold. I have no idea how these films do it, but they do. (Low-E glass also helps reduce ultraviolet light, which degrades carpets and furniture.)

Manufacturers also tint glass to reduce solar heat gain. Highly reflective tinted glass is often used on office buildings because it is very efficient in reducing solar heat gain. But it considerably limits the transmission of visible light, which is why it is seldom used in residences. Gray and bronze-tinted windows reduce light and heat in equal amounts and are the most common in residential use. Blue, blue-green, and green tinted windows offer good radiant heat reduction while allowing in more light. Plant lovers should note that tinted windows transmitting less than 70 percent of visible light will stunt or kill plants inside.

If your budget doesn't allow for coated or tinted glass, you can reduce solar heat gain by orienting the sunroom to minimize direct sunlight in the heat of the day; by positioning roof overhangs to provide shade; or by installing blinds.

Airflow transfers heat in both wanted and unwanted ways. Intentional airflow through vents and screens allows you to mitigate the temperature inside a sunroom with warm or cool air from the outside.

Unintentional airflow, called infiltration, is often a nuisance, adding hot or cold air to a room that is already too hot or cold. Infiltration is a function of how well the window unit (sashes and frame, for example) is constructed, how well it seals when shut, and how carefully it is installed. Working with an experienced, conscientious contractor will help ensure proper window installation, which will minimize, if not eliminate, infiltration around the window unit.

The other insulating criteria are more difficult to assess on your own. Fortunately, a reputable organization has done that for you:

Energy Star ratings are the best way to make informed decisions about window performance. Developed in the early 1990s by the Environmental Protection Agency, Energy Star ratings cover a wide range of products, from appliances to heating and cooling systems. The rating system for windows is administered by the National Fenestration Rating Council (NFRC), a non-profit organization of manufacturers, suppliers, builders, architects, code officials, utilities, and government agencies. The ratings are based on heat loss for the whole window unit rather than just the glass. Energy Star windows are rated in five categories of performance: U-value, solar heat gain coefficient, visible transmittance, air leakage, and condensation resistance.

- U-value ratings generally fall between 0.20 and 1.20. A good rating is below 0.35. (When you compare U-value ratings on windows, pay attention to how it is measured. In the NFRC ratings, the U-value is for the whole window. Some manufacturers list U-values for center of window only, rather than the entire window unit.)
- The solar heat gain coefficient (SHGC) rates a window's ability to block warming caused by sunlight and is expressed as a number between 0 and 1. The lower the number, the better the window is at blocking unwanted heat gain. Look for an SHGC number of 0.40 or lower.
- A visible transmittance (VT) number is the percentage of available light that passes through a window. Higher numbers mean more light in a room. A good rating is around 55.
- Air leakage is a measure of the heat loss and gain by infiltration through cracks in the window assembly. Rates typically fall between 0.1 and 0.3, the lower number indicating less infiltration. Air leakage is an optional rating and a manufacturer may choose not to list it.
- Condensation resistance (CR), a number between 1 and 100, is also an optional rating. Larger numbers indicate less condensation.

Regional differences affect window choice just like they do other building decisions. A window that is very efficient in northern climates may not be the best for southern conditions. The best window for northern winters is one that maximizes solar heat gain in a sunroom while minimizing the loss of warm air from the inside to the outside. Where winters as well as summers are warm, the best window will minimize heat gain from all sources, solar, non-solar, and infiltration.

A label like this indicates an NFRC-rated window. With this rating, a manufacturer can apply for an Energy Star qualification.

In addition to ratings in the five categories just discussed, the Energy Star program rates windows for performance in four climate zones, as shown on the map below.

Energy Star Window Rating Climate Zones

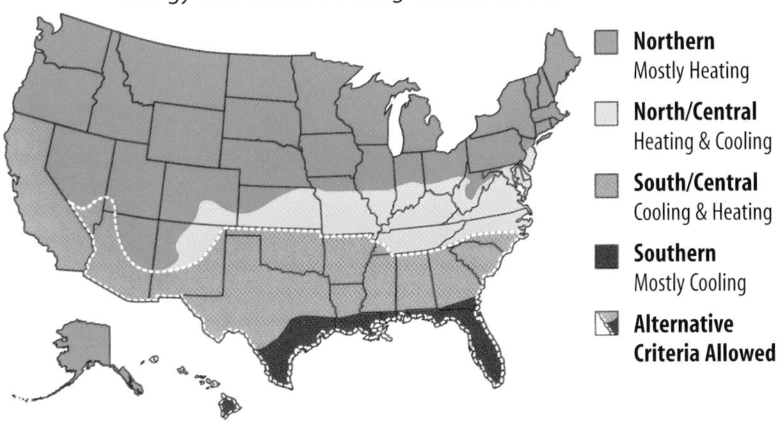

Double-Glazed Insulated Window

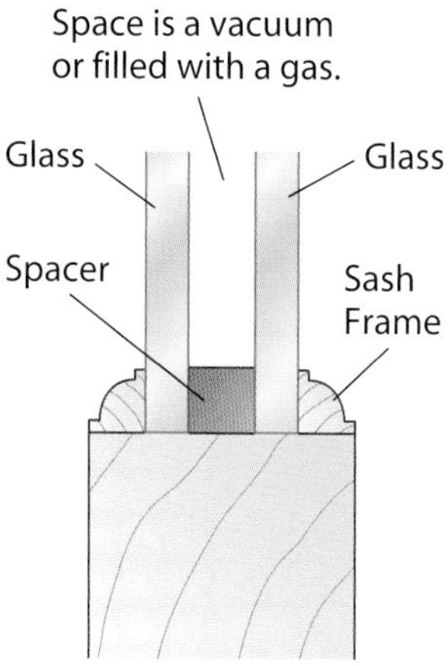

windows cost more than single-pane, but over the long run they can save you money. And from the first day, your sunroom will be much more comfortable.

Insulated windows come in every configuration—double-hung sash, casement, sliding, fixed, and so on—and in every style. You can buy standard sizes or custom built. They are widely available through home stores and lumberyards or ordered through builders or architects. With such variety, choosing sunroom windows can be confusing. Each window manufacturer extols the virtues of its particular brand, citing esoteric terms like "U-value," "Low-E," and "visible transmittance." I've been a contractor for 30 years, and sometimes I feel like a beginner when I'm specifying windows.

False frames attached to these large glass panels create the look of numerous "divided lights."

"The ABCs of Insulated Windows" on page 148, will help you navigate through the competing claims and terminology. If you're converting a porch or building a sunroom from scratch, when it comes to the windows, it is invaluable to have a knowledgeable, trustworthy contractor. If you're looking at manufactured sunrooms, for which everything is supplied, remember that the windows are the most important component—shop around and ask questions before choosing.

The two traditional rooms shown above accommodate lots of glass with different windows. Modified double-hung windows are used above left, while casement windows do the job above right.

Windows: What to Look For

If you're buying your own sunroom windows, look for those with good Energy Star ratings, as discussed on page 149. The window should have a 10- to 20-year warranty,

Glass and Non-Glass Options for Three-Season Rooms

Energy-conscious double-pane insulated glass is ideal for climate-controlled sunrooms. But if you're not heating or cooling, why pay for insulated glass? Firms that manufacture entire sunrooms or three-seasons rooms offer single-pane windows as a cost-saving option. Some of them will sell the windows only, even if you're not buying the whole room package.

Glass isn't the only glazing option for enclosing a three-season room. You should also consider vinyl glazing made of thin, flexible transparent plastic. Vinyl-glazed windows are less expensive than those glazed with glass. They weigh less and are less prone to breaking. Of course, vinyl can be cut with a knife, so sharp objects can damage it. But vinyl glazing is surprisingly resistant to impact. Once, when installing PGT's Eze-Breeze Vertical Four-Track windows, my crew and I tried to break the vinyl, just to see if we could do it. When we threw a baseball at it, the vinyl temporarily deformed, then slowly regained its original shape and tension.

Vinyl glazing is fixed like screening into a groove in an aluminum or hard-vinyl frame. Tinted vinyl glazing is available, which helps cut down on heat gain in the room. Frame finishes, which are usually available in white, light brown (beige) and dark brown (bronze), are baked on and require no repainting. Vinyl-glazed windows can be ordered in sizes up to about 72 inches wide. The PGT Eze-Breeze Vertical Four-Track system has four sashes per window and all four sashes can be slid together, allowing air to move through 75 percent of the opening.

These windows have four horizontal panels, each in its own track, allowing them to be slid up or down to open three-quarters of the window area or any arrangement in between. Instead of glass, the glazing can also be a tough, transparent vinyl.

which indicates quality production and reduced likelihood that the seal in the insulated glass will fail and leak out the gas that lowers the U-value.

Low-E glass is probably worth the extra cost on east- and west-facing windows in northern climates, where heat gain is most pronounced. In southern climates, tinted as well as Low-E glass on south-facing windows might be worth the cost and the reduction of light in the room. When comparing frames, remember that wood, vinyl, and fiberglass have more insulation value than aluminum, unless the aluminum frame is thermally broken. (See "Thermal Breaks" below right.)

As a rule of thumb, the greater the number of separate pieces of glass, the greater the cost. If you like the look of "divided-light" windows (and doors), with lots of little panes framed in a grid, but have a restricted budget, you can buy windows with plastic or wooden frame inserts that give the look of separate pieces of glass.

DOORS

Sunrooms and three-season rooms have similar, but not identical, requirements for doors. Because three-season rooms are unheated and uncooled, they should have insulated doors into the house but not to the outdoors. Sunrooms, heated and cooled like the rest of the house, have opposite door requirements—insulated to the outdoors, uninsulated (or no door at all) into the house.

Doors for manufactured three-season rooms and sunrooms are designed to work with the rest of the structural system. You can specify whether you want insulated or uninsulated, hinged or sliding.

A wide range of commercially available doors are suitable for converted or custom-built three-season rooms or sunrooms. Exterior doors for three-season rooms can be ordinary screen or storm doors. If a sunroom requires an exterior door, I recommend insulated steel or vinyl-clad exterior doors. Other than paint, they require a minimum of maintenance, they seal well, and they come in a variety of sizes and styles. "Full lite" steel doors offer a large area of insulated glass and fit well in sunrooms.

Rooms converted from an existing porch, patio, or deck may already have doors into the house. These may be insulated doors and acceptable for a three-season room. If you like the way they look, there's nothing wrong

Thermal Breaks

Aluminum is a durable material for window and structural frames. It also conducts heat readily. To mitigate this conductivity, manufacturers install thermal "breaks" in aluminum members like those shown in the sunroom below. A nonconductive material, such as vinyl, is sandwiched between the inner and outer parts of the aluminum, breaking the transmission of heat or cold.

The walls of this sunroom are made almost entirely of insulated double doors.

with having an insulated door between a sunroom and the rest of the house.

You may, however, wish to replace a single, hinged exterior door with double patio or French doors. Patio doors have one fixed panel and one that either rolls or swings open. Both panels open in a French door; one is active and one passive. The active door has a regular knob and latch, while the passive door will have a dummy knob, and a footbolt and a headbolt to lock the door in place. The active door latches to the passive door.

Double doors can be made of wood, with the exterior faces clad in maintenance-free vinyl and the interior faces unclad wood, which can be stained or painted to match interior finishes. Maintenance-free (no painting) all-vinyl double doors have good insulating qualities and are available in several colors. If you're considering aluminum doors for a sunroom, those incorporating thermal breaks are best.

Glass in all household doors must be tempered, a safety precaution that prevents serious injury if the glass is broken. You can buy doors with tempered single-pane or tempered double-pane insulated glass.

In general, hinged doors are more energy efficient than sliding doors. But sliding doors keep improving. Aluminum frames with almost no insulating properties have been replaced by more efficient vinyl-clad wooden and all-vinyl models. Sliding tracks have been replaced by rolling wheels built with brushes and baffles to block air infiltration.

ROOFS

The trim and finish surfaces on the outside walls help tie a three-season or sunroom addition to the existing house. But it is the treatment of the roof that often distinguishes a room obviously appended to the side of a house from a room that looks like it has been there all along.

It's worth spending extra time designing, and extra money building, to have a roof that looks right. It once took me a month to find a visually satisfying *and* structurally sound way to tie a roof of an addition to the existing roof. I carried the plan and pictures of the house from job to job and from meeting to meeting, sketching whenever I could. Finally, inspiration struck and in about a half-hour I had the whole thing figured out. The design process often requires some fermentation.

Here are some tips about roof additions to get you started:

- If the house has a roof with gable ends, the addition's roof probably should too. Likewise, if the house has a hip roof, the addition will probably look best with a hip roof.
- The pitch of the new roof should match that of the old.
- The soffits (under the eaves) should be similar, at least, and, at best, tie back into the existing soffits.

Ceilings

In typical house construction, rafters and ceiling joists form triangles that carry and transfer the roof load to the outside walls. A room's finished ceiling is then nailed to the underside of the ceiling joists. This horizontal ceiling is perfectly acceptable for a three-season room or sunroom, but a cathedral ceiling, where the underside of the roof forms the ceiling, is often better. Since these rooms invite the outside in, why not make the inside as voluminous as possible?

To create a cathedral ceiling, you need to eliminate some or all of the ceiling joists. Because the joists tie the two sides of the roof together, some structural replacement is

This sunroom shed roof has been skillfully integrated with the existing roof.

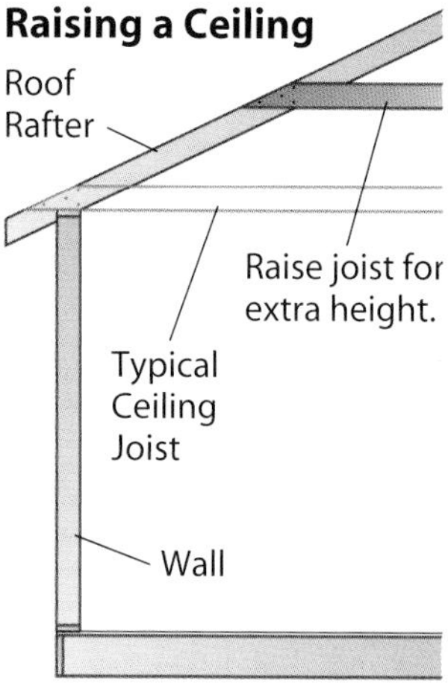

required. Wooden ties higher up on the rafters (as shown at left and in the photo below) can replace some or all joists. I've also seen steel ties or steel cables used to replace joists. If you want to remove all joists, you can install a structural ridge beam, which transfers the load across the roof span to the end walls, thereby eliminating the outward pressure on the sidewalls and the need for joists. The stressed-skin panel roofs common on manufactured rooms form cathedral ceilings automatically. Supported by a structural ridge beam and wall plates, these ceilings need no joists.

The interior finish of a sunroom's cathedral ceiling usually needs to accommodate insulation. For a three-season room, the finish can be as simple as a coating of paint on the underside of the roof sheathing. To give the room a more finished appearance, people usually prefer to cover the rafters or to panel between them.

Post-and-beam walls in a sunroom or three-season room look very good with a timber-framed cathedral ceiling that features hefty rafters and ties on the same spacing as the wall posts. Equally hefty horizontal members, called purlins, connect the rafters. Pan-

eling or other filling between rafters and purlins produces a clean look. Many Southwestern buildings have exposed timber-framed ceilings with plaster or stucco infill and the results look fabulous.

Insulating Ceilings and Roofs

Stressed-skin panel-roof ceilings are already insulated and form their own vapor barrier, so no additional material or work is required.

Insulation for conventionally framed ceilings can be rolled out or blown onto the space between the joists above the ceiling. Heat rises, so the more insulation value you can put above your ceiling the better. Ceilings don't require vapor barriers. Ventilating the space between the ceiling and the roof prevents condensation. This is usually done by vents installed in the soffits and along the peak of the roof. Air is pulled in through the soffit vents and leaves through the roof vents, pulling the moisture with it.

Conventionally framed cathedral ceilings can also be insulated with fiberglass batts between the rafters. The rafters must be deep enough to provide 1 to 2 inches of free-air space between the insulation and the roof sheathing. Soffit and ridge vents move air and moisture through this space to prevent condensation.

A coat of paint is the only interior work required for many stressed-skin panel roofs, above.

Paint blends this cathedral ceiling, opposite, with its surroundings. Note the horizontal ties well above the top of the walls.

Stressed-Skin Panels

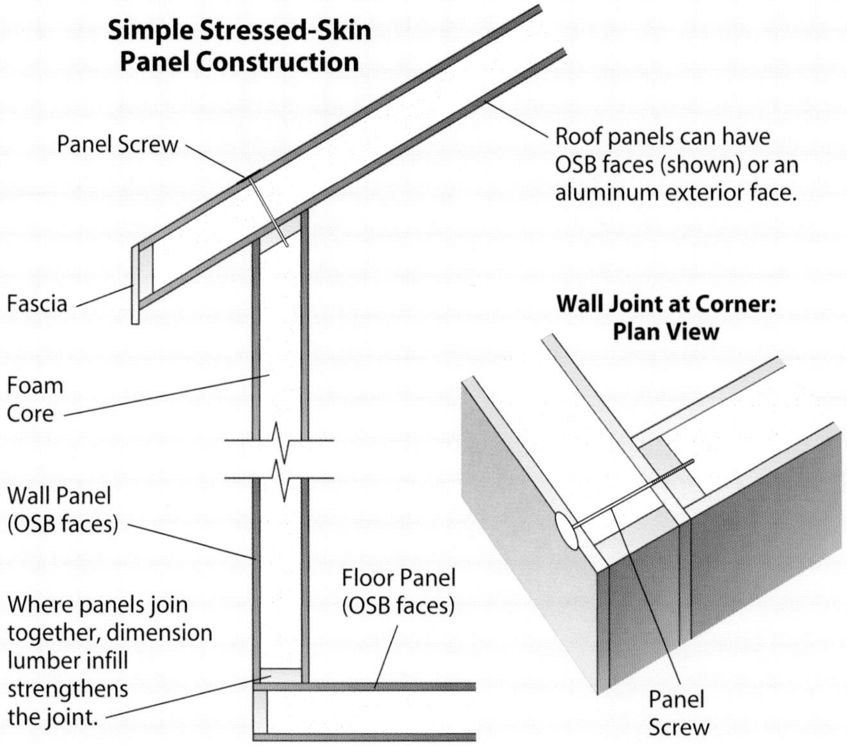

One innovation used to great advantage in three-season rooms and sunrooms is the stressed-skin panel. The panel is a core of expanded polystyrene (EPS) or similar material sandwiched between two sheets of oriented strand board (OSB) or thin aluminum skins. Expanded polystyrene will be familiar to many by its trade name, Styrofoam. What are commonly called stressed-skin panels are actually structural insulated panels (SIPs); we'll use the common term in this book.

Lightweight and very strong, stressed-skin panels can replace load-bearing floor joists and rafters and, in some instances, can serve as walls. In addition to reducing both material and labor costs, stressed-skin panels provide excellent insulation. (The insulation value and cost vary according to the type of core material; EPS has lower insulation value and cost.) Panels range from 3½ to 7½ inches thick for walls, and from 5½ to 11½ inches thick for floors and ceilings. They're usually about 4 feet wide and can be ordered up to 28 feet long. To cover a large expanse, several panels can be joined along their edges with wooden inserts, called splines, or by machined snap-together joints.

Because they lend themselves to large-scale, modular production, stressed-skin panels have been used by room manufacturers and commercial builders for some years. But they are also worth considering for the floor and roof of a custom-built three-season or sunroom addition, where they can provide the same savings and ease of construction for you as for a manufacturer. You or your contractor can order stressed-skin panels through local lumberyards.

Stressed-skin floor panels usually have OSB faces. A slot in the end of each panel is designed to fit over a ledger board bolted to the wall of the house. Depending on the room's size, the panel then rests on a series of beams running parallel to the house. The beams in turn are supported by concrete footings correctly sized for the load.

Stressed-skin floor panels have an additional advantage if the floor will be close to the ground. Panels with aluminum facings, which serve as a moisture barrier, satisfy codes that require the use of treated lumber for wooden members less than 18 inches above ground. Where termites and carpenter ants are problems, codes specify where and how stressed-skin panels can be used near the ground. The critters don't feed on the foam centers, but they can find comfortable housing there and a hidden passage to the wooden feasts available in the home's interior.

For a roof, stressed-skin panels are attached to a ridge beam at the top and are screwed to channel pieces or wooden inserts attached to the top of the side walls, making them ideal for cathedral ceilings. To blend in with an existing roof, panels faced with OSB surfaces are used and tied into the existing roof with conventional framing. Then the valley or wall connection is flashed and the roof shingled to match existing shingles. If the roof either can't or doesn't need to be tied into an existing roof, you can use panels faced top and bottom with aluminum. Just snap the panels together and the roof is complete. You can buy aluminum-faced panels with wood grain or stucco textured surfaces in white, almond (tan) or bronze (dark brown).

Aluminum-faced stressed-skin panels also provide one of the best solutions to the problem inherent in low-pitched roofs, water infiltration. Using 4-foot-wide panels, you can roof a 12-foot-wide room with three panels and only two seams, which are designed to channel water into a gutter. I've been impressed with how few water problems I've had when building low-pitched roofs with stressed-skin panels.

Manufacturers of stressed-skin panels have sometimes exaggerated their products' energy efficiency. In 1993, scientists at the National Renewable Energy Laboratory compared two side-by-side houses, one a stressed-skin home, the other identical, but conventionally wood-framed. Both performed up to the standards of their nominal R-values. This contradicted previous testing by the Florida Solar Energy Center that found a 12 percent to 17 percent energy savings from using stressed-skin panels. The air tightness of the panel construction was marginally better than the conventionally framed house.

Lightweight stressed-skin roof panels need support of a roof ridge and wall only, above and right.

Stressed-skin roof panels can be shingled to match an existing roof, below.

Exterior Insulation for a Cathedral Ceiling

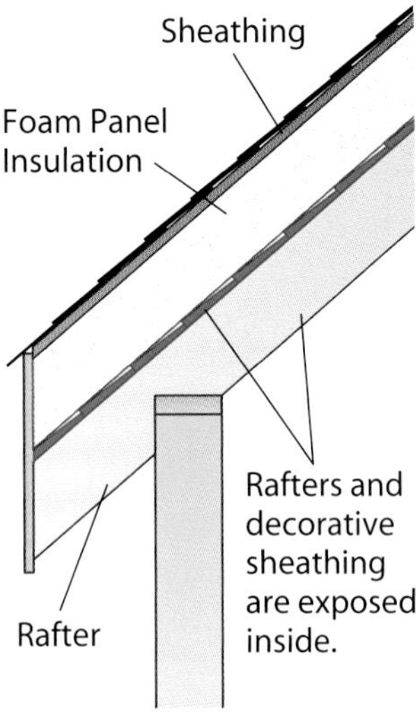

Cathedral ceilings can also be insulated by attaching thick Styrofoam on top of the roof sheathing, as shown in the drawing at left. This system is useful for timber-framed construction, where widely space rafters don't readily allow support of batt insulation.

HEATING & COOLING

The biggest difference between a three-season room and a sunroom is heating and cooling. A three-season room doesn't need any, a sunroom does. And a sunroom, with its glass walls, is almost always the most difficult room in a house to heat and cool efficiently.

There are two basic ways to heat and cool a sunroom. You can tie into the existing heating, venting, and cooling (HVAC) system in your house. Or you can install units to serve just the sunroom.

Using Existing HVAC

If your existing furnace and air conditioner have sufficient capacity and are located close enough to the new sunroom, using them may be the simplest and most cost-effective solution. A heating and air-conditioning professional can determine the sunroom's requirements and the capacity of your existing system. (You can figure these out yourself, but the calculations are complicated, and it doesn't cost much to have someone else do them for you.)

Even if your current system is large enough, using it may not make sense if the room is located at the end of existing ductwork. Pumping enough conditioned air to keep the sunroom as warm or cool as you'd like might cook or freeze other rooms in your home. Because of this, my HVAC contractor recommends against tying into an existing system in most cases.

Supplemental HVAC

You can heat a sunroom (or any other room) on its own with electric baseboard heaters, ceiling-mounted radiant heaters, or with an in-floor heating system. Add a through-the-wall air conditioner if you need to cool the room as well. Or you can install a combination through-the-wall heating and air-conditioning unit.

Electric baseboard units are inexpensive and simple to install; just run the wires and hook them up. I've never found them particularly attractive, but they are easy.

A radiant heater warms people and objects in the room, instead of warming the air in the room like a baseboard heater does. Even if the surrounding air in the room is chilly, you'll feel warm. Radiant heaters are widely used in large, open buildings where it would cost a great deal to heat the large volume of air. Those used in homes are often called cove heaters. They are usually mounted at the intersection of the ceiling and a wall. I like the look of them better than baseboard heaters. After you see them a few times, they'll just blend into the room.

Through-the-wall heating and cooling systems are basically window air conditioners that also heat. They are thinner than window units and more attractive. They mount in a wall rather than a window. Units called "mini-split systems," made by Mitsubishi, Sanyo, and possibly others, are quieter than other systems. They consist of a small fan unit mounted on the wall and connected by freon lines to a small condenser located outside. Used in conjunction with a backup

A fireplace or wood-burning stove may suit the winter needs of some sunrooms or take the edge off chilly spring and fall days in a three-season room.

heating system, you can have quiet, efficient heating and cooling responsive to your specific needs right where you want them.

In-floor heaters, in which fluid-filled tubes or electric heating cables run beneath the floor, are complicated systems to install and are therefore more expensive than the other options. But they're wonderful to experience. Whether the system is electric or fluid, walking barefoot on a heated floor on a cold morning is true luxury.

Humidity Control

Cold winter air is dry, dry, dry, so in northern climes most people humidify the air in their homes. Whether it's from pans of water resting on radiators or a humidifier mounted on the furnace, northerners add moisture to the winter air.

In a sunroom, higher humidity can lead to condensation on the large expanses of colder window glass. Plants add to the problem because they transpire moisture. If it is

Rooms to Order

Manufacturers of three-season rooms and sunrooms supply just about everything you'll need, from floor to roof. Floor systems are either poured concrete slabs or, above ground, stressed-skin panels or conventional joist systems. For walls and roofs, most manufacturers use an aluminum- or vinyl-framed track-and-panel construction system.

The assembler screws the track to the floor. The wall panels slip into the track and snap together in a tongue-and-groove arrangement. Slotted corner posts and a cap on top of the walls tie the entire wall structure together. Wall panels can be almost all window or a combination of window and solid panel. Additional solid panels fill in to accommodate the room dimensions.

With the walls in place, the assembler installs the roof, usually consisting of a ridge beam and snap-together stressed-skin panels. With this system, the roof needs only a ridge cap, eave cover, and gutter fascia to finish it off. Systems are also offered that allow for shingles or other roof surfaces that match or complement your existing home. At each stage of construction, electrical and other services are installed as needed; the various components have been designed to accommodate these services. Then floors, walls, and roof are connected to the existing house. These are usually done by the installer as part of the contract, but you should check beforehand.

An advantage of a manufactured three-season room or sunroom is that once it's assembled it's nearly finished. You may need to install a floor covering; there may be outside steps to build and a door to cut into your home; and you may want to resurface the existing outside wall that is now inside the room. You can contract with the installer for these jobs or you can do them yourself.

With foundation and slab or deck in place, construction proceeds quickly using interlocking framing.

cold enough outside, the condensate will freeze at night and then thaw as things warm up during the day. I've been in sunrooms where water ran down the glass, keeping the window sashes and jambs wet for a good part of the winter.

To avoid rotten woodwork and streaky windows, you need to reduce the humidity in the sunroom, ideally without reducing it to skin-crackingly dry elsewhere in the house. Installing vents in the sunroom and drawing or blowing the moist air out through them unfortunately blows the warm air in the room out, too.

An air-to-air heat exchanger can solve this dilemma. Mounted through a sunroom wall, it pulls in outside air through a baffled system of tubes or heat exchangers that moves the warm inside air across the cold outside air without mingling the two. The wet air on the way out warms the dry air on the way in—thus, air-to-air heat exchange. These units are very efficient, cutting humidity with minimal heat loss.

MANUFACTURED ROOMS

Factory-built three-season rooms and sunrooms, shipped in pieces or sections and assembled on site, have been available for many years. Early versions were often little more than combination windows in simple wooden or extruded frames, and they were not always reliably durable or watertight. Manufactured rooms have come a long way since then, and some are wonderfully well made. Today, manufactured three-season rooms and sunrooms can be erected quickly and offer low-maintenance interiors and exteriors. These rooms are often less expensive than a custom-built alternative.

Precisely machined frames and other components make manufactured rooms efficient to install and durable and dependable in use.

There are many three-season-room manufacturers (see "Resource Guide," page 212) and their research and development engineers are constantly tinkering with ways to make the rooms better. Companies also have design departments that can help you lay out a room, and they usually offer financing, too. The rooms are usually sold through local dealers who are also contractors trained to assemble the rooms. Most manufacturers require installation by assemblers that they have approved.

All the major elements for the room are provided by the manufacturer. (See "Rooms to Order," opposite.) Installation still requires a lot of conventional building skill. The dealer-contractor must correctly size and dig the footings that support the room; tie the room into the existing roof, walls, and floor of your home; cut doorways into interior rooms; and build steps and landings. All this in addition to assembling the room.

So when you're shopping for manufactured rooms, make sure to check out the

French doors lead into this simply furnished enclosed sleeping porch.

dealer-contractor's reputation as an installer as well as the quality and features of the rooms. Ask to see a local installation and talk to owners. If you find a pattern of scheduling problems, poor service or replacement issues, or leaking rooms, you should find another dealer-contractor.

The Process

The first step in purchasing a manufactured room typically is a visit to your home by the dealer-contractor to show you brochures and company information and find out what features you're interested in. Then he or she will design the room from the company's offerings, sometimes with the help of the manufacturer's design team. The package you buy includes the room and installation. I don't know of any manufacturer who will allow a homeowner or unauthorized contractor to install their rooms.

Depending on the time of year and the manufacturer, it can take a month or two to manufacture a room. If the dealer-contractor is really good at scheduling and the company is good at keeping shipping dates, he or she may do some of the preparatory work before the room package arrives at the local warehouse or on site.

Once the room arrives, it will go up quickly. A model with a simple shed-style roof that attaches to the side of your house and requires no shingling may take just a day or two. A room with a cathedral ceiling, gable-end windows, and a roof that needs to be tied into an existing roof will take longer but will still go up fast.

INTERIOR DECORATING & FURNISHING

Being somewhere between a porch and a room in your house, a three-season room can be furnished anywhere along the spectrum between the two. A sunroom can, in addition, be indistinguishable from other rooms in the house.

For both three-season rooms and sunrooms, you can tie the style and design into a theme you have running through the rest of your house. Or you can branch off in an entirely new direction, exploring the room's connection to the outdoors, for example. ■

This carpeted sunroom is as elegant as the rest of the rooms in this house.

CHAPTER 5

Conservatories

A conservatory is the ultimate sunroom—it has glass walls and a glass roof. At its best, a conservatory provides an almost seamless transition between the outdoors and the comforts of home. It can be a striking setting for an evening meal, a comfortable spot for morning coffee, a distinctive room for entertaining, or the perfect place to curl up with a book. And a conservatory is the only room in your house where you can enjoy an indoor garden or gaze at the stars.

A RICH HISTORY

Conservatories have been around for as long as there has been flat glass with which to glaze them. Europeans have erected glass rooms and buildings since the sixteenth century, first to protect delicate plants from inclement weather and later as rooms for entertainment, too.

The largest conservatory ever built housed the Great Exhibition of 1851 in London. Dubbed the Crystal Palace, it covered 17 acres with almost one million square feet of glass. Some 4,000 tons of cast iron and more than half a million cubic feet of timber held the glass in place.

Tucked into a corner, bottom left, or tethered loosely to the house, top left, these European-style conservatories are distinctive additions to large traditional homes.

A conservatory is part of this striking home's access to the outdoors, above. The modest lean-to conservatory below offers sunny comfort in often inclement Vermont weather.

Like its more modest Victorian counterparts, the Crystal Palace was very expensive. Innovations in manufacturing and technology have reduced the cost of conservatories, putting them in reach of ordinary homeowners. You can spend several hundred thousand dollars on a custom-built conservatory, but today $20,000 will buy and install a handsome manufactured conservatory.

DESIGN

Before you decide to build a conservatory, you need to understand and come to terms with its fundamental nature. Built almost entirely of glass, a conservatory collects a lot of sunlight and gets hot. And on a cold winter's night, it can lose heat as quickly as it gains it during the day. Insulated windows help, but even the best of them insulates little better than $1\frac{1}{2}$-inch-thick dry wood.

If you build a conservatory, you must accept that you're going to spend money, perhaps quite a bit of it, heating and cooling it. If expense is a concern, ask the room's manufacturer for estimated utility costs. If you're custom building, your gas or electric company should be able to provide an estimate based on the design. If the estimates are sobering, consider a sunroom instead, which offers more scope for insulation.

If you can live with the estimates, your reward will be a room that will likely become the favorite in your house, a venue for peaceful contemplation as well as for boisterous gatherings and lively conversation.

As for porches and sunrooms, a conservatory's orientation with respect to the sun is

The architectural details of the custom-built conservatory opposite blend the structure into the rest of the home. The sleek, curved look of the manufactured conservatory below offers a different experience from the rest of the house.

A small conservatory can make a secondary entrance a more welcoming spot, above and left, while it provides all the function and comfort of a larger version.

The main entrance shown opposite showcases a conservatory structure and spiral staircase to wow and welcome visitors.

important. A location with less exposure to mid-to-late afternoon summer sun will ease utility bills. If you want a morning room, make sure it catches or avoids the morning sun, depending on your preference.

It is likely, however, that choices of exposure are limited by the layout and orientation of your house. If the optimal spot in relation to the sun is adjacent to a bedroom, you'll probably look elsewhere, unless you have in mind a private conservatory. Often people locate a conservatory where the flow of traffic and activity in the home tends toward the out-of-doors. Located off the rec room or living room, a conservatory adds to the range of indoor activities. Or it might adjoin a dining room, offering a place to enjoy an aperitif before dinner or a cup of coffee afterward, surrounded by nature.

A glass room raises concerns about privacy, of course. On an acreage, what you can see from your conservatory may be your main consideration. In town, enhancing your view may take second place to screening your neighbor's view. Well-placed plantings, both inside and out, and privacy fencing can help you invite in nature without inviting in the neighborhood.

Considerations of size are somewhat different for a conservatory than for other rooms. You'll want to maintain scale with the rest of the house. And you'll want to accommodate all the desired activities. But you also need to consider that a room with transparent walls feels larger or smaller than an ordinary room, depending on its surroundings. Stake out the room's footprint on its intended site, and spend some time imagining what a space created by glass walls and, effectively, no ceiling or roof will feel like.

Conservatories can be built in just about any architectural style. Manufacturers offer models that reflect Victorian, Georgian, Edwardian, or Mediterranean design elements. Custom-built conservatories come in shapes and sizes restricted only by the structural requirement of having glass all around.

Because of all the glass, particularly the glass roof, it is difficult to blend a conservatory addition seamlessly into an existing

house. A custom-built design can echo structural details and materials; a manufactured room relies mostly on proportion to appear "at home." In the end, a glass room is a glass room, and it may be easier, and certainly cheaper, to appreciate it for its distinctive features, rather as you might treasure an eccentric aunt or uncle.

Mahogany provides rich warm tones in the interior of the custom-built conservatory below. The wood is also an excellent choice for weather resistance and durability.

MATERIALS

Conservatories consist largely of two elements, glass and the frames that support it. I'll discuss the choices available for both. The range of framing materials is fairly wide. But there are choices to be made for glass, too.

Materials for Frames

Early European conservatories, like the grand houses they adorned, were often constructed of cut stone or masonry walls with timber-framed roofs. Then, as now, this type of building was very labor-intensive. As conser-

The factory-painted cedar structure shown above requires relatively little maintenance while adding to the airy feeling of the room. The steel frame below needs occasional painting but is no less charming.

vatories began to feature on humbler residences, less expensive and more easily fabricated frameworks of wood or iron housed all the glass, sometimes resting on low stone or brick walls.

For aesthetic and practical reasons, wood is an ideal conservatory material. A conservatory is a transitional space between the outside and the inside, and wood is a common element in both environments. Outdoors, it is part of nature; indoors, it is warmer (both literally and figuratively) and more inviting than stone or iron. Practically, wood is a good natural insulator, and it is versatile. It can be

shaped and joined to form arches, curves, and just about any other geometric form. And it can be sawed, shaped, drilled, glued, and fastened on site, with tools and techniques familiar to a large number of skilled artisans. A wood-beamed conservatory in the soft tones of cedar or fir and sheathed in glass is about the perfect combination of nature and technology.

Wood requires some maintenance, both inside and out, but with regular upkeep it can last for centuries. And wood ages well, becoming more beautiful as it acquires the patina of weather and use over the years.

Along with wood, iron was, until the mid-twentieth century, the most common framing material for conservatories. Small in cross

The conservatory at left uses conventional stud framing and standard windows and doors in the walls. Custom-made double-pane glass panels fit into a wood-framed roof.

The owner-built conservatory on this page comprises a wood frame, four sets of inexpensive sliding-glass doors, and a modular roof system with double-paned glass. A thermostatically activated fan helps control the heat.

Conservatory or Greenhouse?

If you intend to grow many plants in your conservatory, you should make sure it can provide the conditions the plants (and you) prefer. Unless you're growing desert plants, be prepared for high humidity. Temperate and tropical plants transpire a great deal of water. Plants can also be fussy about temperature.

In a mild climate, mechanical ventilation may be sufficient to handle humidity and temperature requirements. Where winters are cold, you'll need to control the heat and the condensation caused by wide variations in outside and inside temperatures. An air-to-air heat exchanger, discussed in Chapter 4, may do the trick. (See "Humidity Control," page 161.) But you may need something more sophisticated. If your conservatory is going to be a surrogate greenhouse, consult with a greenhouse expert during the design phase of your project.

section and very strong, iron allowed glass to form most of the surface of a wall or roof. Iron lends itself to mass production, and it was once the ideal material for large conservatories. Iron has one serious drawback as an outdoor material—rust. Unless painted regularly, it quickly looks awful and begins to deteriorate structurally.

With twentieth-century advances in the low-cost production of aluminum, this strong, lightweight, and rustproof metal has become a popular material for conservatory frames that are mass produced in the factory. Aluminum is too difficult to shape and join on site for use in custom frameworks. Many custom-built conservatories, however, incorporate manufactured aluminum window units in a wooden structure.

Aluminum's main drawback is its high heat conductivity—it is a poor insulator. To overcome this problem, manufacturers make frame components by sandwiching a non-

SMART TIP

Always Crystal Clear. Technology may offer hope to people who want a conservatory but don't like to wash windows. Several manufacturers now produce "self-cleaning" glass. A microscopically thin coating of titanium dioxide on the glass absorbs UV light, producing a "photocatalytic effect" that breaks down organic dirt. The coating also makes water "sheet" off the glass rather than bead up on it. Combined, the two properties loosen dirt and allow rain or a good hosing to rinse the window clean and without streaks.

conductive material between two aluminum extrusions, one forming the component's outside face, the other its inside face. This "thermal break" slows the transfer of heat. The aluminum comes in a small range of permanent colors (no painting required) and, sometimes, textured surfaces.

The most recent addition to conservatory frame materials is a rigid polyvinyl chloride (PVC), often reinforced with aluminum. PVC provides good insulation without thermal breaks, needs no painting, and is relatively inexpensive. Like aluminum, it can be ordered in several colors and surface textures.

Know Your PVC

If you're considering a PVC-framed conservatory, be sure to note the differences between one manufacturer's PVC and another's. The PVC itself may vary in thickness, and the frame members into which it is formed may vary in overall thickness. There may also be differences in internal reinforcement. Make sure PVC roof members, especially, are reinforced with aluminum or galvanized steel.

Although the windows above and opposite are similar, the round-headed panes impart a Victorian feel, in contrast to the Georgian-style divided lights.

Glass

Regardless of the framework, a conservatory's comfort and longevity depends on its glass. Until recently, single-pane glass, fragile and of little insulating value, was the only option. In addition to its own drawbacks, single-pane glass was fixed into the iron or wooden frame with putty-like caulking that hardened and cracked with age, leaking air and water into the structure.

If you live in a climate that is mild year-round, like Santa Barbara's, for example, single-pane glass is an option. But elsewhere it makes little sense to build a conservatory without insulated glass. The discussion on glass in Chapter 4 applies to conservatory glass as well. (See "The ABCs of Insulated Windows," page 148.) I recommend gas-filled double-pane units with a Low-E coating. Tinted glass, which filters the sunlight, seems counterintuitive in a conservatory, where visibility is of primary importance. If you have a fat wallet and you like cutting-edge technology, you might explore "smart windows," which can alter their characteristics depending on the temperature or sun intensity.

Non-glass materials are also available for conservatories. Many manufacturers offer polycarbonate, a lower-cost alternative to glass. It is virtually unbreakable, but it is less clear than glass.

Blinds

Old-fashioned technology also offers help in controlling heat gain and loss and mitigating the damaging effects of sunlight. Blinds have been used on windows since at least ancient Roman times. They are offered by most conservatory manufacturers and can be fitted to custom-built rooms. Blinds protect upholstery and carpets from degradation by ultra-

violet (UV) light. They can reflect back much of the radiant heat penetrating the glass in summer and help retain heat in the winter. And blinds can offer privacy year-round.

When evaluating blinds, think of them as another layer of window. How well do they reflect sunlight? How well do they retain heat? How much light passes through them? Do they reflect or transmit UV light?

Three styles of blinds are commonly used in conservatories: roller blinds, pleated blinds, and Roman blinds. Many kinds of blinds or curtains will function on the glass

A glass roof opens your home to the heavens, center. But there are times when a little shade is a good thing. Roof blinds, below and far right, are essential for moderating sunshine and heat gain in a conservatory.

walls, but blinds for the roof must fit inside tracks on the frame to keep them from sagging. Manufacturers of conservatories and conservatory windows often offer blind and track systems. Some systems have electric operators, which is a great help in a large room.

Roller blinds, the least expensive style, work just as the name implies. A length of fabric is rolled up to allow sunlight in and rolled down to block it. Some roller blinds have a reflective backing that reflects even more of the sun's heat back outdoors.

Pleated blinds form a stack of narrow fabric pleats as they are drawn up. The fabric can be treated to repel dirt and moisture and to increase reflectivity and resist UV degradation. Some manufacturers offer a range of fabric densities that allow differing amounts of light into the conservatory when the blinds are drawn. Pleated blinds are available in a wide range of colors and can be ordered to fit windows of almost any size.

Roman blinds, used in British conservatories since the Victorian era, are a variant of pleated blinds. The blind consists of a wide strip of fabric that has been hemmed at intervals to form horizontal pockets for narrow strips of wood (or other stiff material). To draw the blind, you pull on a cord that connects the strips and the fabric forms a series of overlapping folds as it is raised.

CONSTRUCTION

Building a glass room is a job for only the most advanced do-it-yourselfers or professionals. A custom-built conservatory requires a full range of carpentry skills, as well as engineering calculations to determine wind and snow loads on the glass roof and walls. Manufactured conservatories, like factory-built sunrooms, are almost always sold and installed by licensed franchisees.

Even if you're not building the conservatory yourself, it is useful to be familiar with basic conservatory construction to help you with a custom contractor or to inform your purchase of a manufactured room. Apart from the glass roof, there are few differences between a sunroom and a conservatory.

Glass: Safety and Security

Most building codes in the United States require tempered glass in a conservatory. Created by a process of controlled heating and cooling, tempered glass is considerably more resistant to breakage by wind and projectiles than ordinary annealed glass. And when it does break, it fractures into many small pieces rather than a few dangerously jagged shards.

A glass room may not seem terribly secure, but with tough tempered glass and appropriate locks on the doors and windows, a conservatory will be as secure as the rest of your house. If you need more assurance, consider an alarm system that detects broken glass.

Foundations and Floors

Just like the humblest porch, a conservatory requires a solid foundation. Because of all the glass, any movement due to a poor foundation can have disastrous consequences. A variety of foundation and flooring systems, from traditional joist-on-foundation walls to innovative stressed-skin panel systems, are suitable for conservatories.

A concrete floor, poured on the ground or on an aboveground platform (both, of course, with proper footings), is a solid and very practical choice. A concrete slab provides a stable support for the structure and can also serve nicely as the primary floor. For a conservatory that functions as a rec room or plant room, a smooth, hard, steel-troweled surface will suffice. The concrete can be stamped and colored to look like slate, other types of stone, or brick.

Alternatively, the slab can serve as a subfloor on which you can lay any flooring. Stone, brick, or ceramic tile are the best choices. Wood and carpet are possibilities, but they can perform poorly in constant sunlight. Tile is a popular choice because it is attractive, durable, and easy to clean and

Positioning the floor of a conservatory addition a step below the existing floor in an adjacent room is easier to accomplish than attempting to align the two at the same level. Note that the double doors allow the conservatory to be closed off to help control heat gain and loss.

maintain. And it offers a mind-boggling range of choices, from brightly colored glazes to hand-crafted rustic patterns from Spain, and from 1-inch squares to giant tiles almost 2 feet across.

Utilities

A room with glass walls presents few options for electrical service (outlets and lights) and plumbing (tap and drain for a plant room or a wet bar). If the conservatory foundation will be a ground-level concrete slab, the electrical conduit and pipes for plumbing are incorporated in the slab. In-floor heating, an excellent system for conservatories, is also installed at this time. (See "In-Floor Heating," page 186.) If the floor of the room is to be above ground, the mechanicals can run under the decking and be installed after the room is built.

If the conservatory has glass panels that rest on a low framed or masonry wall, electrical services can be run from the slab into the wall and outlets and fixtures mounted on the wall. If the conservatory has floor-to-ceiling glass, the electrical outlets can be installed in the floor. Many manufacturers include special runs for electrical services in the framework. This is easier to do with metal than wood components.

In-Floor Heating

In-floor heaters are more expensive than other options, but they're wonderful to experience. There are two common systems. In one, electric coils or mats are laid on a subfloor underneath a finish floor of wood or tile. The other comprises a series of fluid-filled tubes embedded in a concrete floor. The fluid is heated by an external unit and pumped through the coils. Both systems take advantage of the natural tendency of warm air to rise. There are no noisy blowers, no dust blowing around, no ducts to place furniture around, no return air vents on the walls, and no cold spots. Just quiet heat. Whether the system is electric or fluid, walking barefoot on a heated floor on a cold morning is true luxury.

Both systems have advantages. A fluid system warms up and cools off faster than an electric system, and it is usually cheaper to run. An electric system eliminates the pumps, heaters, and manifolds required by a fluid system. If you want to use the concrete slab as a finished floor, a fluid system is usually the only option. Neither system heats up or cools down quickly. So if the weather warms up, the floor will continue radiating heat when you would prefer it not to. Conversely, if the weather suddenly turns cold, it will take the floor system a while to catch up.

Both systems can be used beneath a variety of flooring materials. Stone, ceramic tile, and brick are ideal. Engineered hardwood flooring and laminate flooring are possible but less suitable, perhaps, for a conservatory. Solid hardwood or softwood flooring is not a good choice over radiant heat; the drying effects of the heat could cause it to shrink and crack.

In-Floor Heating: Fluid System

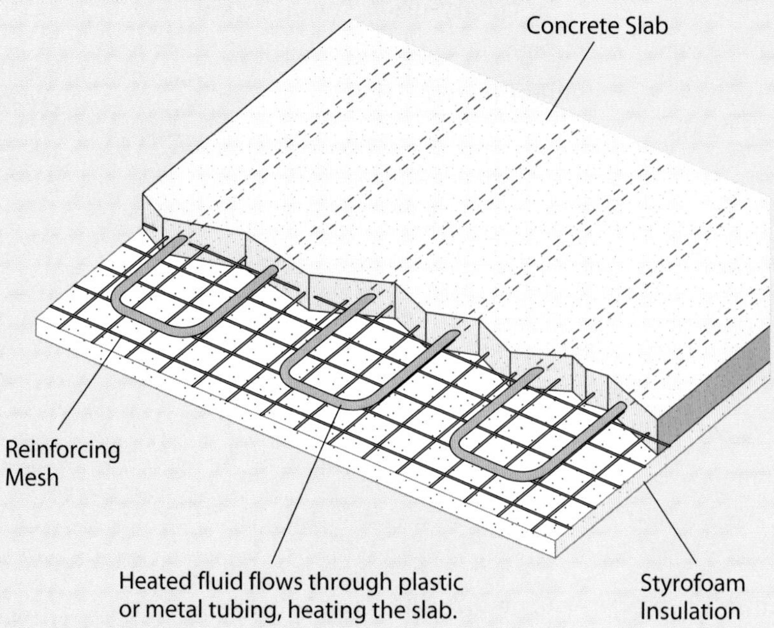

In-Floor Heating: Simple Electric System

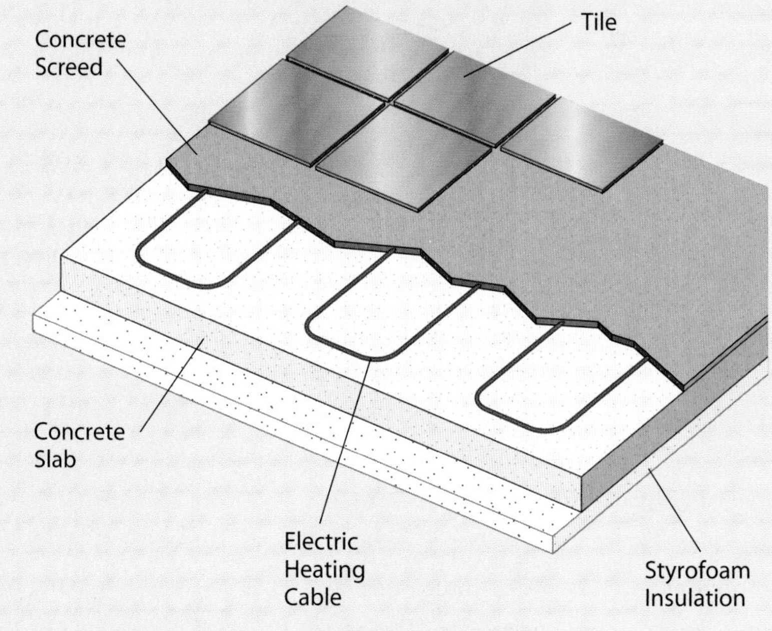

Walls and Roof

A custom-built conservatory can combine a variety of structural features and materials, as mentioned earlier. It might be framed entirely of dimension lumber to house custom-built or standard factory-made wall panels or windows. It might incorporate custom-fabricated aluminum or steel elements in the framework.

A manufactured conservatory, on the other hand, arrives like a giant kit, with all the parts ready for assembly by a specially trained crew. The "kit" can go up remarkably fast. Aluminum or vinyl frameworks for walls and roof screw or bolt together. The glass can be fixed into the wall system at the factory or on site. Roof panels are hoisted in place and installed once the frame is up. Fewer manufactured conservatories are made of wood, a beautiful material, but more difficult to design and build in kit form.

HEATING & COOLING

Supplying a conservatory with heating and air conditioning isn't difficult or necessarily expensive to install. Paying the monthly bills may be another matter.

Other than installing insulated glass, there are few options for insulating a conservatory. If you're building on a concrete slab, insulate beneath it, installing a plastic moisture barrier to prevent ground water from wicking up through the concrete.

In-floor heating is, to my mind, the best and most comfortable heating for a conservatory. But it is expensive. The heating system options discussed for sunrooms also work well for conservatories. (See "Heating & Cooling," page 160.) Tying into your existing forced-air HVAC system makes even less

Copper flashing, above, transitions into a short section of standing-seam roof where this conservatory attaches to an existing wall.

An old-fashioned heating system—a wood stove—keeps the conservatory shown below toasty in winter.

Windows and roof vents can moderate the temperature in a conservatory very effectively. The roof vents shown above are opened and closed by cylinders filled with paraffin that expands and contracts as the temperature changes.

sense for a conservatory than for a sunroom. Electric baseboard heaters or a through-the-wall heater-air-conditioner, or a "mini-split system," are better choices.

Conservatories have even more glass than sunrooms to foster condensation, so it's very important to provide enough venting. One rule of thumb suggests that the area comprising vented windows and doors be at least 15 percent to 25 percent of the floor area in the conservatory. Most conservatory roofs are also vented at the ridge and sometimes along the eaves.

FURNISHING

Because a conservatory is an enclosed space, there are few restrictions on furniture or furnishings beyond recognizing the problems of mildew and deterioration that can occur if humidity isn't controlled.

As for style, there are really no rules beyond those of personal taste for a room devoted to enjoyment. Your furnishings will, of course, reflect the uses of your conservatory. For some, it's a bright and sunshiny dining room; for others, a sitting room; and for yet others, a mini gym.

Traditionally, rattan and wicker furniture were staples for conservatories. And they still are. They provide an easy transition from outside to in, reflecting the purpose and theme of the room itself. Not too formal, not too casual, just comfortable and inviting. Rattan, in particular, holds up very well in humid conditions. Cushions, pillows, throws, and blinds provide opportunities for splashes or bands of color. ■

Wicker looks as good in a modern conservatory as it does in an ornate Victorian setting.

DEWALT

CHAPTER 6

Repair & Maintenance

Despite all the sales hype you hear about "maintenance-free" manufactured sunrooms or products for remodeling your porch, nothing is maintenance free. Someone, sometime, will have to paint, patch, or caulk, or things will eventually fall apart. Maintenance free means less maintenance, perhaps, or different maintenance, but it is still maintenance. And maintenance often shades into repair. This chapter examines common maintenance and repair needs and how to meet them.

Aluminum valley flashing sheds water at the intersection of a hipped porch roof and the house roof.

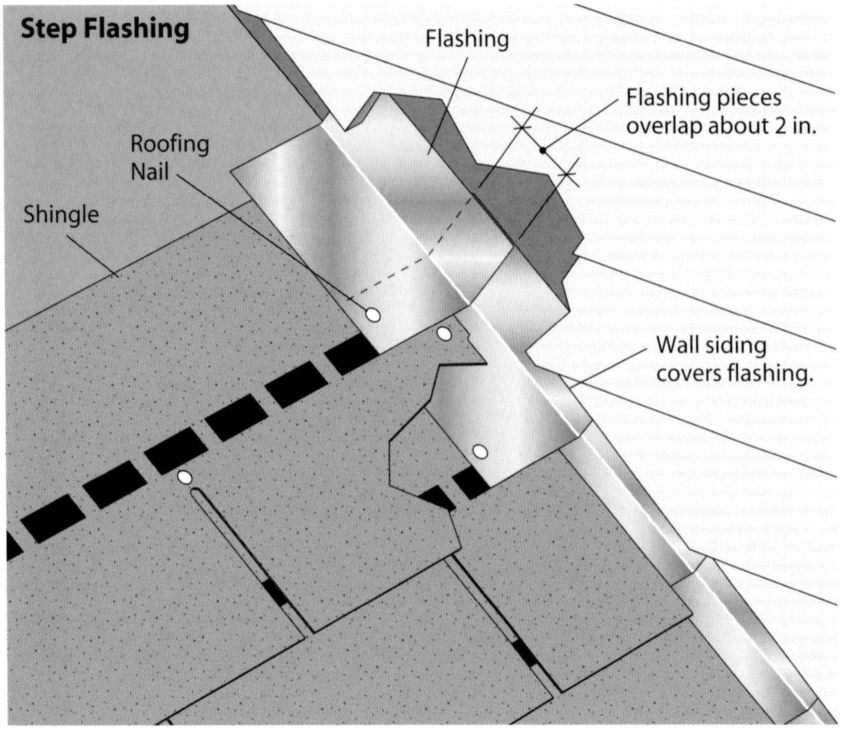

Step flashing, as shown in the drawing above and photo below, forms a much tighter water seal than strip flashing.

ROOF FLASHING

The primary joints in a porch, sunroom, or conservatory, and those between these structures and the existing house, should rely on flashing, not caulking, to seal out weather. This is particularly important for joints between a roof and a house wall. Flashing is a piece of metal, usually aluminum, that fits under shingles and against any surface adjacent to the shingles, so that water flows over the shingles and down the flashing.

There are two common methods of flashing a roof-to-house wall joint. Simplest is a continuous piece of metal running the length of the joint beneath the shingles. Unfortunately, water can work its way under the shingles unless the joint is caulked. In cold-weather environments, the freeze-thaw cycle can push ice up under shingles, where it will thaw and create leaks that are very difficult to track back to their cause.

Better is to step-flash the joint. In this technique, individual pieces of flashing are inserted beneath each course of shingles (and under lap siding) so that the flashing as well as the shingles are lapped at each course. You or your builder should also incorporate some form of ice and water shield in the original construction in any area at risk of water intrusion. The shield won't guarantee leak prevention, but it's a deterrent.

CAULKING JOINTS

Caulk is intended to bridge and seal gaps that would otherwise admit water, dirt, or other possibly damaging substances. It is supposed to do this while clinging to two often dissimilar materials that expand and contract with every change in temperature. Here in

Work with Nature

To lessen the maintenance and repair you'll need to do at a later date, do your best to work within nature's constraints when you build or renovate a porch, sunroom, or conservatory:

- Water flows downhill. The steeper a roof or valley, the easier it sheds water. Avoid incorporating flat roof areas or roof-to-valley junctions with little or no slope.
- Ultraviolet light degrades certain materials, such as plastic and paint. Research thoroughly before you buy.
- Different materials expand and contract at different rates during the freeze-thaw cycle. Don't depend on a caulk joint between different (or even the same) materials as a permanent weather seal. Use mechanical seals (flashing and tight-fitting or overlapping joints, for example) wherever possible.
- Dirt, moisture, mold, mildew, termites, carpenter ants, and decay are all part of a natural process, and they will, without malice or respite, break down whatever you build into the smallest possible pieces as quickly as they can. So design and build to avoid creating nooks and crannies in the roof (and other parts of the structure) where water can back up, where airborne debris can accumulate, or where mold, mildew, and fungus can grow.

Nebraska, for example, seasonal temperatures vary by 70 degrees or more. We've recorded temperature swings of 100 degrees in 24 hours.

Squeezed into gaps that continually widen or narrow, caulk is prone to failure. In the summer, the material on both sides of the gap will heat up and expand. The gap narrows, and the caulk squeezes out. Then in the winter, as the surrounding materials cool and contract, the caulk adheres to one side and comes loose from the other, causing a leak.

Given what caulk is subjected to, it is remarkable that it holds up as well as it does. While you shouldn't rely on caulk instead of a well-designed and well-constructed structure, caulk certainly is effective for maintenance and repair.

Where two different roofing materials meet, careful flashing of the joints between them is particularly important, as shown in this porch and screened three-season room addition.

Regular Checkups

At least once a year, check the major horizontal and vertical joints in your porch, sunroom, or conservatory. Horizontal joints include those above and below windows and doors and between the floor or roof and the side of the house. Vertical joints are those on the sides of windows and doors and between room walls and the side of the house.

Vertical joints are usually caulked during construction, as much to tidy up the appearance as to fill problematic gaps—leaks aren't usually a problem along vertical joints, where water can't easily collect. Nevertheless, if you find cracked or missing caulk along a vertical joint, repair it before it does become a problem.

Gapped or cracked horizontal joints can lead to more serious problems. The best repair is to create a mechanical seal, usually by fixing existing flashing or adding new flashing. Caulking these areas is a quicker and cheaper alternative, but one that should not be counted on long term.

For porches and three-season rooms, floor- or deck-to-wall joints are often caulked rather than flashed. Flashing doesn't look very good on wood flooring, so those joints are usually caulked or, if they're protected from the weather, left open. Joints involving concrete slabs are almost always caulked.

Caulk seals the vertical joints between the metal columns, walls, and windows on this custom-built sunroom.

Choosing Caulk

Retail stores stock a range of different caulks for different needs. Generally speaking, there are caulks made of acrylic, latex, silicone, and urethane, alone or in different combinations.

For most exterior uses, I've had the best luck with urethane caulk, and I recommend it to homeowners. It doesn't have all the color options some of the other types have, and it can require some shopping to find, but I use it for most joint repairs because of its durability and tenacious grip. It's also paintable, unlike some caulks. I also use butyl-rubber caulks. They're dependably water resistant and durable, and they're paintable, too.

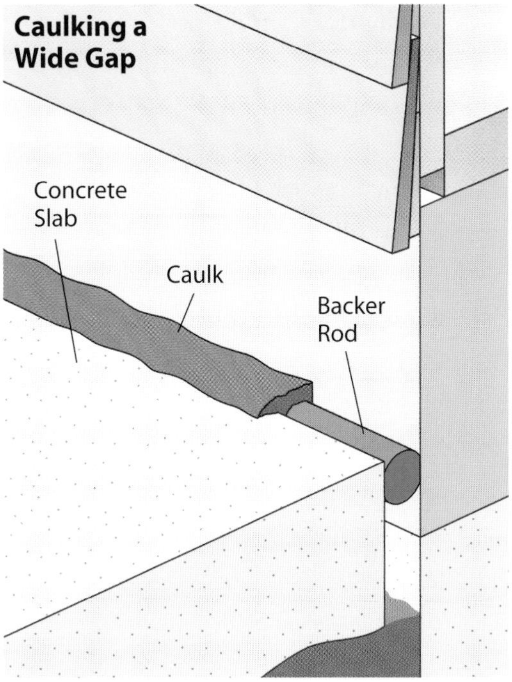

Urethane and butyl-rubber caulks are not as easy to use or clean up as latex or acrylic caulk. If they get on your clothing, they will stay there. Where the caulk adheres to your person, it will eventually wear off, or you can scrub it off with a solvent.

Silicone caulk works well indoors around tubs and sinks, but I haven't had good luck with it outdoors, where it doesn't seem to adhere as well as other caulks.

Poor caulking results aren't always the fault of the caulk. Proper selection (the right caulk for the job) is important. Read the manufacturer's specifications before you buy the caulk. Special caulks are made for a variety of needs, including vertical or horizontal joints and gap width.

Caulk for vertical applications is fairly viscous and won't sag while it is curing. Self-leveling caulks are made for horizontal applications. As the name suggests, the caulk, like water, seeks its own level. A word of caution: use self-leveling caulk only in level areas and where you can block off the ends of the gap to be caulked. The caulk is "runny," and it will run into holes that may appear small to you, and disappear. The first time I used self-leveling caulk, I pushed backer rod into a gap between a concrete slab and a garage and gunned in the caulk. The joint looked great, so I went inside to get paid. When I took another look at my "completed job," the caulk had disappeared. Problem was, the backer rod hadn't fit tight enough in the joint and the syrupy caulk leaked away.

In addition to special caulk, wide gaps often require "backer rod." These polyurethane ropes come in a range of diameters that can be squashed into cracks to back up the caulk.

Applying Caulk

Caulking is not a difficult procedure, but remembering a few simple things will produce better and longer-lasting results. Manufacturers specify the temperature of application, the drying time before painting, and whether application to a damp surface is acceptable. Be sure to read the label. For easier application, buy the caulk in tubes that fit into a racheted caulk gun. You can buy the gun almost anywhere the caulk is sold.

SMART TIP

Caulking Claims. Caulk is commonly rated by the number of years it is supposed to last: 10 years, 15 years, 25 years. I have no doubt that the caulk itself will last as long as advertised; indeed, it will probably be found intact in some post-civilization landfill. Unfortunately, it won't be stuck to anything, having come loose from its moorings before its claimed life span is up as a result of too many freeze-thaw cycles.

Making a Clean Caulk Joint

The most difficult part of tooling a caulk joint is keeping the caulk from building up on your finger and smearing on each side of the joint. Wiping inevitable smears as you go is seldom successful. Before caulking, I tape each side of the joint, leaving ⅛ inch or so of each surface exposed. Then I gun in the caulk and tool it with my finger. The residual caulk accumulates on the tape, which I pull off right away. The result is a smoothly tooled joint with nice, crisp edges. This technique is time-consuming and somewhat difficult on a stone or brick facade, but it is worth the effort.

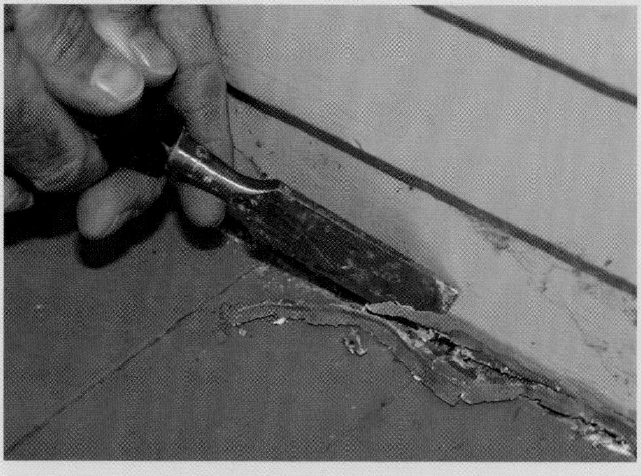

Cut away old, cracked caulk with a sharp chisel. Clear debris out of the joint. Sweep the surfaces clean.

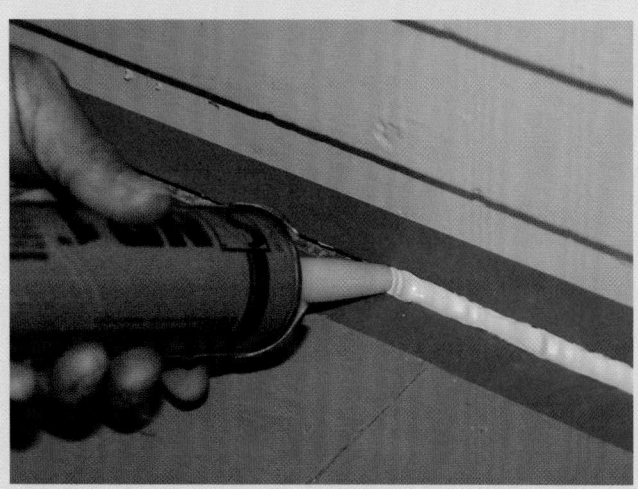

Protect adjacent surfaces with blue, easy-release masking tape. Squeeze caulk into the joint with a caulking gun.

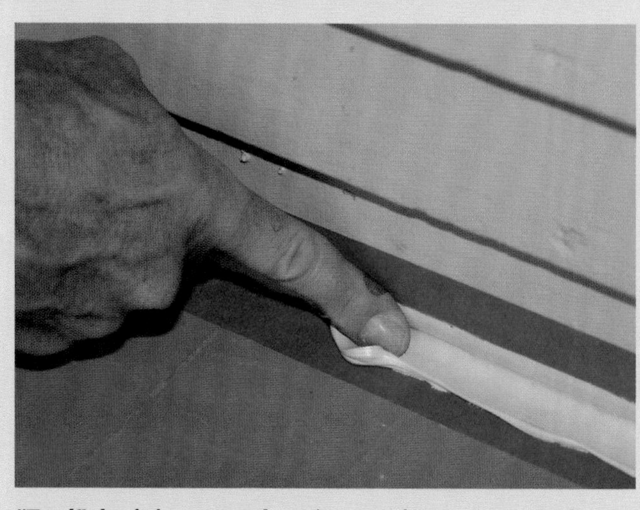

"Tool" the joint smooth with a wet finger. Remove the masking tape to produce a neat, smooth caulked joint.

Before applying the caulk, prepare the joint carefully. When you're caulking a joint for the first time (no previous caulk being evident), remove loose material with a paint scraper, and then make sure the surfaces are free of grit and dust.

If the joint has been caulked previously, remove any caulk that has pulled away from either adjacent surface. It's tempting to just push new caulk into the joint, but this often only masks an underlying problem. Dig out all the old caulk, and clean the joint by scraping both sides of the joint well. Brush the remaining dirt and debris from the joint.

When the joint is clean, fill any portion that is wider than about ¼ inch or more with backer rod (depending on the gap-filling capacity of the caulk as specified on the tube). On a very good day, I can sometimes squeeze a smooth, neat joint right out of the caulk gun. Usually, however, I need to "tool" the joint to make it look professional. The tool is just my finger, so I always have it with me. First I wet the finger with water or a solvent, depending on the type of caulk. The moisture helps produce a smooth finish and limits the amount of caulk that sticks to my finger. I slide the finger down the length of the joint, pushing the caulk firmly against both surfaces of the joint to produce a neat, attractive seal.

Tool the joint very soon after you caulk it. Most caulks "skin over" quickly once they're out of the tube, and the skin makes it difficult to produce a smooth surface. Resist the urge to "touch up" here and there.

FOOTING PROBLEMS

Inadequate or faulty footings are at the root of numerous porch problems. (And those of three-season rooms and sunrooms converted from faulty porches.) The footings don't support the deck, which begins to sag. In consequence, every joint in the structure opens. The joints exposed to water will leak, and things will begin to rot.

Code-compliant footings on porches, sunrooms, and conservatories rarely develop problems. But they can do so as a result of soil conditions that were undetected at the time of construction or a record-breaking winter that drives frost deeper than the footings required by code.

Perimeter Footing

As the name implies, this footing runs continuously around the perimeter of the porch or room. If you suspect that an inadequate perimeter footing underlies a sagging porch, a little exploratory probing or digging will usually provide an answer. If the soil is soft enough, push a steel rod into the ground alongside the footing to see how far down it extends. Digging a small hole alongside the footing is even better. You can then excavate further, if need be, to see how the footing was poured or laid.

If a footing isn't deep enough (check with the code department for the required depth) or it has deteriorated, you can choose from four options for a remedy:

You can maintain what you've got and hope it doesn't get worse. Do what you can to keep water from infiltrating around the footing to prevent further freeze-thaw damage or shifts in soft soil. Replace caulk where needed on porch joints, and replace boards as they split and move. This is not an altogether bad solution if the porch is in reasonably good shape and has been so for some years. And it is certainly the cheapest option.

The next level of intervention is to stabilize the footing where it is without releveling the porch or room. This is primarily a job for professionals. Using special equipment and

Masonry porches and most sunrooms have perimeter footings. Footing problems are common on older porches built before stringent code requirements.

This porch renovation in Vermont uses an ingenious traditional method of post footing that employs concentric pipes. Supporting each post is a pipe, or rod, that rests on a stone set beneath the frost line. An outer pipe (white PVC here) sheathes the inner pipe, from the rock to just above ground. As the ground moves with the freeze-thaw cycle, the outer pipe moves with it, but the inner pipe, and the deck, remain stable.

engineering techniques, they will excavate alongside the footing and attach steel brackets to it. Next, they will drive in pilings or "screw in" helical piers and attach them to the brackets. The pilings or piers are engineered to transfer the load from the existing footing to undisturbed bearing soil.

The third option uses the same piling or pier technology to raise the footing to a level position and stabilize it there. This can be expensive and is not always possible without risking damage to the porch or room.

The most thorough, and usually most expensive, option is to replace the footing and to level and plumb the porch or room on top of it. This requires installing temporary supports for the structure above the footing while the footing is removed and replaced. For a porch or room with an old-style footing that extends only a foot or so into the ground, this is really the only option, as there is no way to stabilize a shallow footing.

Post Footings

These footings are not continuous, and support only corners or other specific points on the structure. They're usually made by digging a hole down to the frost line and filling it with concrete. A wooden post or masonry pier rests on the concrete.

Older wood-framed porches were often built on undersized or shallow post footings, and often the result is leaning posts. (Masonry porches require a perimenter footing.) Fortunately, faulty or inadequate post footings are simpler to remove and replace than a perimeter footing. After erecting temporary supports for the roof and floor, you (or your contractor) can remove the post, column, or pier. (If you want to reuse the support, remove it carefully.) Then remove the existing footing, and pour a new one at the correct depth. If you are doing this yourself, be sure to consult with an engineer or your town's building department to find out the correct footing size and reinforcement. Finally, reconstruct and reinstall the pier, post, or column.

PORCH DECKS

With appropriate maintenance, porch decks (or three-season-room floors) can last a long time. Solid-wood flooring that is properly ventilated and regularly painted, sealed, or varnished can last for decades. Concrete porch decks require very little maintenance to last even longer.

And if maintenance slips and a few boards deteriorate or unexpected damage occurs, replacing boards is possible if you have some basic tools and a little patience. (See "Repairing Solid-Wood Porch Decking" on page 202.)

Paint and Other Coatings

Paint or varnish is essential for traditional tongue-and-groove pine flooring, which lacks natural rot-resistant qualities and needs the protection of a wear-resistant coating. Decks or floors made out of rot-resistant cedar planks or many of the harder tropical woods now sold for decking and flooring may not need protection from weather or wear. But unless you want a weathered, well-worn look, some sort of regularly maintained coating, even just a sealer, will be necessary.

You can buy special porch-floor paint designed to withstand the rigors of foot traffic and constant weather-related indignities. If you want a clear or stained finish, sealers formulated for uncovered decks will also work on porches. Clear film finishes, such as polyurethane, are less often used. Spar varnishes, long used for wooden boats, are more

A leaning pier is a telltale sign of faulty footings. Column and pier lean out where they meet and lean in at top and bottom. The extent of the problem is also obvious from the size of the gap between the porch deck and pier.

A nicely painted porch floor looks good even when it is just a simple brown, above. The caramel-colored paint on this slab deck complements the brick and limestone railing wall, below.

suitable. Consult with a paint supplier for other possibilities.

If you're concerned about a slippery surface, you can buy paints and finishes with additives that produce a nonslip surface.

You can touch up worn areas on an "as needed" basis, but it's best to recoat the whole porch deck on a regular schedule. A thorough cleaning beforehand will ensure a durable, well-adhered finish. Scrape or sand off all loose paint and grime. If the existing surface has a gloss finish, sand it or use a chemical deglossing agent to ensure that the new paint adheres to the old.

Even without a gloss surface, it's a good idea to sand the entire deck to make sure all loose paint is removed. You don't need to sand down to bare wood. A random-orbit sander works well. I don't recommend using a belt sander (the small hand-held models or the commercial floor sanders). Unless you're an experienced operator, it's too easy to gouge the wood with them. After sanding, sweep off all the dust.

A few tips about applying paint or a film finish: pay special attention to coating the exposed end grain of the porch boards that usually overhang the first step. That's a high-

SMART TIP

Uncarpet Your Porch. If your porch deck is carpeted, take the carpet off. If you're thinking of carpeting your porch, take some deep breaths and think how much it will cost to replace the whole floor when moisture in the carpet rots the underlying wood.

wear area and unprotected end grain is more likely to absorb water than the surface face grain.

Avoid painting a deck when it is exposed to the sun. Even if the day isn't particularly hot, paint exposed to direct sunlight can dry too fast to produce a smooth, even coat. And the paint might not cure properly. If the day is windy, erect a tarp windbreak to keep dust and debris from blowing onto the wet surface. It takes a little time, but it can make a better job.

Concrete porches are often painted, though they don't really need protection from weather or wear. Concrete tends to produce dust, which is one reason—other than aesthetics—for applying a finish. Buy paint or sealer specially formulated for concrete, and make sure the surface is clean before painting. Apply a primer-sealer to give the top coats better adhesion.

The little maintenance required for composite flooring and decking varies according to manufacturer, so be sure to follow their instructions.

Ventilation

In addition to maintaining a surface coating on a wooden porch deck, you need to ensure that the deck is properly ventilated. Even though it may be protected by a roof, a porch deck gets wet. Moisture migrates up from the ground, snow whirls around it, and rain blows or seeps in.

Even if moisture leaks through the gaps between boards and soaks the wood, it won't cause problems as long as the bottom surface of the deck can breathe and dry out. You can plant shrubs and flowers around the porch and install skirting; just don't seal off the area under the porch.

To prepare a deck for painting, first scrape off loose paint.

A random-orbit sander with a coarse sanding disk will ensure that all loose material is removed.

Pay special attention to the end grain of porch deck boards, an area that wicks up water if not sealed well.

Repairing Solid-Wood Porch Decking

Broken, rotted, or cracked boards in a porch deck should be replaced. This is relatively easy for square-edged face-nailed boards, which can just be pried up with a wrecking bar and replaced with new boards.

Replacing tongue-and-groove blind-nailed boards is more work. To remove the old boards, saw one of them down the middle with a portable circular saw. Then pry each half out with a bar or a hammer (or both). Adjacent boards will pry out fairly easily. If you're replacing only a portion of the board, cut partway through the board above a floor joist and chisel through the waste side of the board at the cut.

Next, pull nails and remove fragments of the tongues or grooves from the exposed edges of the bordering pieces. Then fit in new boards, blind-nailing as you go, until the last board. Cut the bottom flange off the grooved edge. Slip the tongue into the groove of the adjacent board, and face-nail near the edge with the single-flange groove. If you can slide the new boards in from an end, you don't need to cut away the flange.

Be aware that the new floor boards may be a different width or thickness than the old. If they are thinner, you can add thin strips to the joists to make the surface of the floor flush. If they are wider, you can rip-saw them narrower. Cut material off the groove side, and remember to adjust the width of the tongue as necessary to make a tight joint.

New boards that are narrower than the old are trickier. If you're replacing boards that run from the front to the back of the porch, you can cut a narrow piece to fill the gap between the last new board and the adjacent old board. If you're replacing only part of the length of a board or boards, you can space small gaps evenly. Or you can have flooring milled to match the original. Wide gaps are unsightly and prone to damage. Once the new flooring is pieced in and the face-nails set, fill the nail holes with exterior-grade filler. Then prime and paint to match the rest of the porch deck.

Saw along the length of the boards to be removed, above, and chisel a clean end, below.

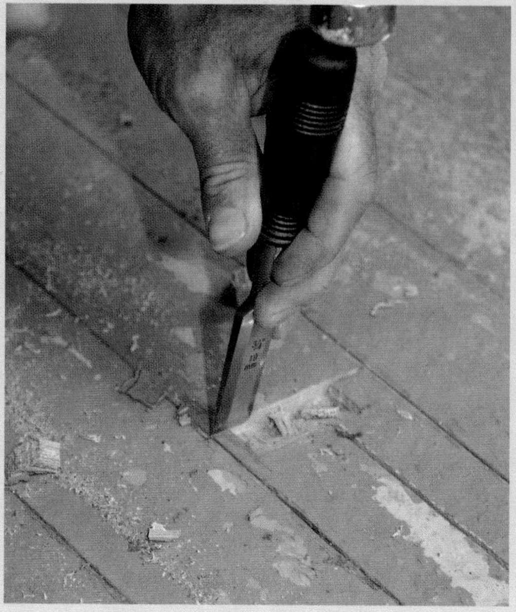

SUNROOM & THREE-SEASON FLOORS

Floors in sunrooms and three-season rooms can be maintained in the same way as the floor in any other room in your house. (Some three-season rooms are more like porches than sunrooms and will need similar maintenance.) You might have the occasional wet floor to deal with if someone leaves the windows open on a rainy day. Of course, that could happen in any room. It's just that a sunroom can ship in a lot of water. If so, you may need to pull the carpet back to allow the subfloor to dry, decreasing the chance for mold and mildew to grow.

Some sunrooms or three-season rooms and most conservatories have hard-surfaced floors of concrete, tile, or stone. These floors require very little maintenance.

If you're not removing the entire board, chisel a clean end on the remaining piece.

Slide in new boards from the end, above. Here, the groove in a new board engages an old tongue.

When the new boards are fitted and nailed in place, trim the ends flush with the old boards, above.

A concrete sunroom or three-season room floor, like a concrete porch floor, will benefit from a special sealer to eliminate the dusty residue of unsealed concrete. You'll need to reapply the sealer from time to time.

Tile floors may require touch-up grouting, and occasionally a tile will loosen and need to be reset. It's a good idea to save some of the original tile and grout in the rare case that a tile breaks and needs to be replaced.

CEILINGS & SUPERSTRUCTURE

Protected from sun, rain, wind, and wear, a porch ceiling requires little maintenance beyond keeping its paint or finish looking good. A roof leak can damage the ceiling. In fact, ceiling damage is often the first indication of a leaky roof. Fixing the leak is the first requirement. After the leak has been repaired

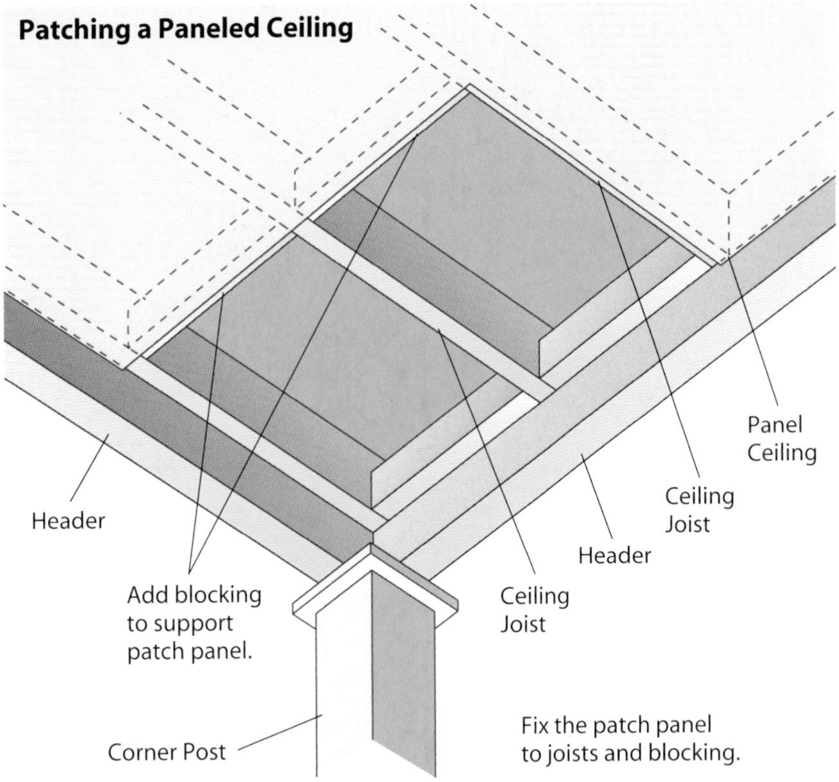

Battens hide the joints on this paneled ceiling. If you repair a paneled ceiling that doesn't have battens, you might add them to the entire ceiling to help mask the patch.

and everything has dried out, you may need to refinish the ceiling. If the leak has gone undetected for a long time, the ceiling damage may be extensive, and the ceiling may require patching or replacement.

Ceilings with tongue-and-groove boarding or solid-wood planking can be repaired as outlined earlier for similar flooring material. The repair will be a bit more difficult because you will be working overhead. Plywood or other ceiling panels can also be patched by cutting out an area bounded by ceiling joists on which to fasten the patch. (See the drawing at left.)

Older porches with gable roofs sometimes suffer "sagging span." That is, the header that runs between one outside post, column, or pier and the other wasn't made large enough, and it (and the gable framing) sags under the weight of the roof and gable it supports.

The simple solution is to add one or more post supports under the header to cut the length of the span. At the same time, you can try to jack up the header enough to remove the sag from the gable framing. This is usually futile in older homes where the framing members have "set" in the sagging configuration. It's safer to stabilize the header than to try to remove the sag. Whether the new supports are posts, columns, or piers, they'll be carrying a load and will therefore need a code-compliant footing.

Another way to straighten a sagging gable is to replace the header. This requires considerably more work, including at least partially dismantling the gable framing. But a correctly sized glue-laminated beam (a stack of lumber glued together to form a beam) or steel beam will certainly solve the problem.

The relatively modest span under this porch gable is amply supported and shows no sag. Note how the large roof overhang protects the superstructure above the columns from weather.

POSTS & COLUMNS

The most common problem with wooden porch posts or columns is rot. (Leaning posts and columns are usually the result of footing problems.)

Solid-wood posts will rot if the base of the post is in frequent and lengthy contact with water. Posts that run from the ground up should be fixed to an aboveground-level concrete footing with a yoke-like metal fastening that doesn't trap water. You can retrofit a yoke to a post fairly easily (and pour a new footing if necessary), if you can support the weight of the porch with a jack while you're doing the work. You should install naturally rot-resistant posts and treated wood posts the same way, even though they would take a very long time to rot.

A more common problem occurs with classical or built-up columns that rest on a concrete slab or porch deck. Most of these columns are hollow and have ventilation holes that allow them to "breathe" from the bottom up through the top. Column bases should be relieved so that they allow water and air to flow under them.

I've replaced many rotten wooden column bases that sat directly on a slab or deck. No matter how you caulk or seal around the wood, the base will eventually rot. And without proper ventilation to allow air up through the column, the columns can also rot.

Replacement isn't always necessary. If rot is minimal and the problems are cracks or missing pieces, it's possible to reconstruct the damaged parts. Sometimes I shape and insert wooden patches. But often I make the repairs with epoxy. Areas that are rotten but workable I consolidate with a liquid epoxy. To build up areas where pieces are missing, I use a special two-part epoxy with a putty-like consistency. While it is workable, I sculpt it roughly to shape. Once the epoxy hardens, I shape it with woodworking tools to match the original.

If rot or damage is extensive, it is best to replace the base or, if necessary, the whole column. Many companies that manufacture architectural columns also sell bases, capitals, and shafts for repair work. They stock a range of styles and sizes and also custom-make parts, so you should be able to obtain a more-or-less identical replacement.

After pouring new footings for this porch, the piers were relaid and the distinctive mortar joints of the original re-created.

Fixing a Column

Whether you're replacing part or all of a column, you'll need to support the roof (or whatever the column is supporting) while you work. Floor jacks or a constructed framework will do the job.

The photographs show a replacement of a badly rotted column base. The new

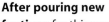

A jack supports the roof while the column is being removed and repaired.

cast-stone molding is supported by an aluminum base plate. Even though the aluminum will never rot, it is relieved in order to allow air to circulate through the wooden shaft and capital to prevent condensation and rot.

The original base plate and molding were rotten. But the damage extended only about ½ inch up the column shaft. Fortunately, the decorative fluting on the shaft stopped several inches above the bottom of the shaft, so it was possible to saw off the rotten part without compromising the look of the column.

The base molding and portion of a matching pilaster shaft had also rotted. (A pilaster is a half column attached to a wall.) I replaced these with wooden parts made by a local shop to match the originals. Once painted, the column and pilaster matched nicely, despite being made of several different materials.

A cast-stone molding and aluminum base plate will replace the badly rotted column base, above. Rotten wood at the bottom of the column shaft is removed, below.

Repairs to the matching pilaster were made of wood in a local shop.

The striking paint job above highlights elaborate details while it protects the railing.

Caulk doesn't solve the footing problem that caused the separation of the railing and pier shown above.

RAILINGS

Handsome railings can give a porch real eye-appeal. But they take a lot of abuse, particularly wooden railings. Railings have dozens, sometimes hundreds, of pieces. All are subject to the ravages of seasonal movement as the wood expands and contracts with changes in temperature and humidity. And the numerous joints that hold the pieces together provide access for rot-inducing water and voracious insects.

The only defense you can mount against the effects of weathering is a well-maintained coat of paint. If the paint is intact and you begin to see open joints, the problem is likely to be found in the footings. Well-built railings should fit tight to columns and walls, and any subterranean movement will open those joints.

If the joints are gapped, fix the footings before tackling the railings. If the footings are fine, or you've fixed them, the railings may need little more than a coat of paint. Scrape off loose paint; check for cracking at joint lines; lightly sand the areas where you'll need to touch up; and then paint. Small gaps or cracks can be caulked, but keep your eye on them—if they widen, check the footings.

If you find rotten or damaged parts, you can replace them or, if the damage allows, repair them with epoxy, as discussed in "Fixing a Column," page 206. Simple railing parts can be duplicated by most local woodworking shops. More complex moldings or balusters may be harder to duplicate locally. Manufacturers of columns may also stock replacement railing parts or be able to custom-make them.

Railings made of composite materials shouldn't need much maintenance, though you might need to tighten screws if joints begin to loosen. If a part is damaged, however, it's likely to need replacement; it's hard to repair plastic. Buy from an established manufacturer, and it will be a lot easier to find replacement parts if you need them.

WINDOWS

Windows in a three-season room, sunroom, or conservatory should be maintained in the same way as the windows in the rest of your house. Keep the frames and moving parts clean, and don't build up coats of paint on sash edges or areas on the frame that contact those edges.

Condensation is often a problem on sunroom and conservatory windows. When water runs down the panes onto a vinyl or aluminum frame and sill, it's just messy, not harmful. But if water stands on wooden sashes, frames, and sills, it can damage the finish or, at worst, lead to rot. Keep an eye out for condensation, and wipe the woodwork when you see that it is wet.

The most common repair for windows is replacing broken glass. A hail storm is a conservatory owner's nightmare. And while insulated windows are a wonderful energy-saving and comfort-producing innovation, they are not easy or cheap to repair.

One of the trade-offs we as a society have made in acquiring technically advanced low-maintenance products is that we're no longer able to fix what breaks. If an errant baseball breaks a single-pane glass window, you can buy a piece of glass and reglaze the sash yourself, or you can have the local glass shop do it

SMART TIP

Stockpile Window Parts. If you buy new windows for a sunroom or conservatory, order some spare parts at the same time. Ask the window installers what sort of replacements they regularly make, and lay in a supply before you need them. Aluminum latches, for example, are wonderfully corrosion resistant but not very durable, so over time you're likely to need replacements.

Fixing broken glass in a double-glazed manufactured conservatory almost always requires a replacement panel from the factory.

for you. But if an energy-efficient, double-glazed, gas-filled insulated window breaks, you may well have to replace the sash, because the glass is factory installed with factory gaskets, factory gas, and factory caulk.

Insulated glass in fixed-sash sunroom or conservatory windows and roof panels can often be replaced as a sealed unit without a new frame or sash. Most movable-sash windows require full sash replacement.

While your replacement sash or glass is on order, you'll need to put up a temporary weather shield until it arrives. If you're not in a high-wind area, a piece of 4-mil plastic duct-taped securely to the frame should suffice. If security is an issue, screw a piece of plywood to the old sash. If it's winter, caulk it in place to block the draft.

This overgrown shrub is too close to the base of this porch, creating a humid sanctuary ideal for insects and making it difficult to see early signs of damage that they might cause.

INSECT DAMAGE

Insects are another reason to keep excess moisture in check in a porch, sunroom, or conservatory. Carpenter ants and termites thrive in moisture.

Carpenter ants don't actually eat wood, but they tunnel into it, leaving only a thin wooden shell as they remodel your residence to fit their needs. When they're active, carpenter ants leave telltale piles of sawdust, hence the name.

Termites do eat wood. They live in underground colonies and are attracted to houses for the food found in the framing. Termites leave dust too, but it's much finer. The more obvious signs of termites are the earthen tunnels they build to traverse exposed surfaces. Termite tunnels are thin, hardened dirt umbilicals connecting the ground to some wooden member of the house.

Most building codes require at least an 8-inch strip of exposed concrete foundation above the ground, which provides an initial barrier to termite infestation or at least a no-termite's-land where you can see whether you have visitors.

Vigilance is the first line of defense against carpenter ants and termites. Be on the lookout for piles of sawdust or mud tunnels clinging to a wall. I encourage people to keep plantings a couple of feet back from the foundation. Foliage provides excellent cover for unwelcome visitors. Place plants so that you can easily see the exposed strip of concrete at the base of the foundation and any tunnels built on it.

If you find evidence of termites or carpenter ants, call an exterminator. As much as I dislike chemical warfare, it's about the only way to deal with wood-eating insects.

TRACKING DOWN LEAKS

Despite your best efforts at maintenance, your porch, sunroom, or conservatory may spring a leak. Before you can fix it, you have to find its source.

Although you can see where water is leaking into a porch or room, there's no guarantee that the source of the leak is at the same spot on the outside. Tracking down a leak often requires a little "forensic maintenance."

Some leaks, such as those generated by a failed window seal, for example, can be fairly easy to track down. It can be much more difficult to discover exactly where water is penetrating a roof. The most likely places are the valleys and where flashing makes a transition from one angle or one material to another. But water seeping into a cracked flashing near the top of a roof may appear on the inside above a window at the base of the roof.

If you've crossed off the obvious candidates—missing shingles, torn or separated caulk joints, broken window seals—enlist water itself in the search. Starting outside near the spot where the leak appeared on the inside, run water from a hose on the side of the house or on the roof. Slowly move the hose up until you can re-create the leak. (Water, of course, always flows downhill, so it makes no sense to look lower than the height of the leak.)

Place the hose above the starting point, rather than shooting a stream of water at it from below. You can inadvertently create temporary leaks by driving water too far under flashing or shingles.

Take your time. It can take a while for water to wend its way to its outlet site. If you move too fast, you'll have moved past the point of entry when the leak appears inside.

Fluid-system in-floor heating, ideal for sunrooms built on concrete slabs, requires monitoring of boilers and pumps on a regular basis.

IN-FLOOR HEATING

Electric in-floor heating costs more to run than a fluid system, but it requires almost no maintenance. In a fluid system, the pumps that circulate the water through the tubing and the boiler that heats the water require regular maintenance.

Some systems use additives in the water to inhibit corrosion or to provide cold-weather protection. Where additives are required, you'll need to check the mixture (or the system pH) periodically. Some systems also require a complete draining and refilling every five or six years.

Pumps use water to lubricate the bearings, and most pumps have a life span of about 10 years. Boiler maintenance varies by manufacturer. Most system installers offer a yearly contract to clean the heat exchanger and adjust the burner. ■

RESOURCE GUIDE

The following list of manufacturers and associations is meant to be a general guide to additional industry and product-related sources. It is not intended as a listing of products and manufacturers represented by the photographs in this book.

MANUFACTURERS AND BUILDERS

These companies design and build three-season rooms, sunrooms, and conservatories. Some produce manufactured rooms, others custom build; some do both. Many also offer accessories.

Buena Vista Sunrooms
8274 Quincy St.
Ventura, CA 93004
Phone: 800-747-3324
www.sunroom.com

Colebrook Conservatories
152 Stillman Hill Rd.
Winsted, CT 06098
Phone: 800-356-2749
www.colebrookconservatories.com

Four Seasons Sunrooms
5005 Veterans Memorial Hwy.
Holbrook, NY 11741
www.fourseasonssunrooms.com

Hampton Conservatories
490 New York Ave.
Huntington, NY 11743
Phone: 877-884-8500
www.hamptonconservatories.com

Hostetler Patio Enclosures, Inc.
319 S. E St.
Milford, NE 68405
Phone: 800-809-8674
www.sunroomsbyhostetler.com

Marston & Langinger
117 Mercer St.
New York, NY 10012
Phone: 212-575-0554
www.marston-and-langinger.com

Patio Enclosures, Inc.
Phone: 800-480-1966
www.patioenclosures.com

PGT Industries
1070 Technology Dr.
Nokomis, FL 34275
Phone: 877-550-6006
www.pgtindustries.com

Renaissance Conservatories
132 Ashmore Dr.
Leola, PA 17540
Phone: 800-882-4657
www.renaissanceconservatories.com

Tanglewood Conservatories, Ltd.
15 Engerman Ave.
Denton, MD 21629
Phone: 410-479-4700
www.tanglewoodconservatories.com

TEMO Sunrooms
20400 Hall Rd.
Clinton Township, MI 48038
Phone: 800-344-8366 ex. 250
www.temosunrooms.com

Westview Products
1350 S.E. Shelton St.
Dallas, OR 97338
Phone: 800-203-7557
www.westviewproducts.com

Internet Sources

Additional conservatory and sunroom suppliers and manufacturers can be found at these web sites:

Conservatories Online
www.conservatoriesonline.com/finda-suppusa.htm

The Directory of Garden and Leisure Buildings
www.gardenbuildings.com/directory/Conservatories/United-States

WINDOWS AND DOORS

These manufacturers produce stock and/or custom-built windows, doors, and related items.

Andersen Windows
100 Fourth Ave. N.
Bayport, MN 55003
Phone: 800-426-4261
www.andersenwindows.com

C & S Distributors, Inc.
1640 Rte. 5
South Windsor, CT 06074
Phone: 800-842-7307
www.c-sdistributors.com

Energy-Efficiency Window Ratings
Energy Star
1200 Pennsylvania Ave. NW
Washington, DC 20460
Phone: 888-782-7937
www.energystar.gov

Gerkin Windows & Doors
P.O. Box 3203
Sioux City, IA 51102
Phone: 800-475-5061
www.gerkin.com

JELD-WEN, Inc.
P.O. Box 1329
Klamath Falls, OR 97601
Phone: 800-535-3936
www.jeld-wen.com

Jim Waters Corp.
419 Manchester Rd.
Poughkeepsie, NY 12603
Phone: 845-452-6310

Marvin Windows and Doors
P.O. Box 100
Warroad, MN 56763
Phone: 888-537-7828
www.marvin.com

Master Window Systems, Inc.
2060 DeFoor Hills Rd.
Atlanta, GA 30318
Phone: 404-355-5844

Pella Windows & Doors
102 Main St.
Pella, IA 50219
www.pella.com

PVC Industries
107 Pierce Rd.
Clifton Park, NY 12065
Phone: 518-877-8670
www.pvcindustries.com

Tri-State Wholesale Building Supplies
1550 Central Ave.
Cincinnati, OH 45214
Phone: 513-381-1231
www.tri-statewholesale.com

Self-Cleaning Glass

Sunclean
PPG Industries
One PPG Pl.
Pittsburgh, PA 15272
Phone: 412-434-3131
www.ppg.com

Activ
Pilkington Glass Co.
www.pilkington.com

Screens

Screen Tight
One Better Way
Georgetown, SC 29440
Phone: 800-768-7325
www.screentight.com

DECKING AND FLOORING

These manufacturers produce flooring suitable for porches, three-season rooms, sunrooms, and conservatories.

Composite

ChoiceDek
Weyerhaeuser Co.
Phone: 800-951-5117
www.choicedek.com

EverGrain
Epoch Composite Products, Inc.
P.O. Box 567
Lamar, MO 64759
Phone: 800-405-0546
www.evergrain.com

EverNew
CertainTeed Corp.
750 E. Swedesford Rd.
Valley Forge, PA 19482
Phone: 800-233-8990
www.certainteed.com

Geodeck
Kadant Composites, Inc.
8 Alfred Cir.
Bedford, MA 01730
Phone: 877-804-0137
www.geodeck.com

Nexwood Industries, Ltd.
1327 Clark Blvd.
Brampton, ON L6T 5R5
Canada
Phone: 888-763-9966
www.nexwood.com

TimberTech
894 Prairie Ave.
Wilmington, OH 45177
Phone: 800-307-7780
www.timbertech.com

Trex
Trex Company, Inc.
Phone: 800-289-8739
www.trex.com

Veranda
Universal Forest Products
2801 E. Beltline
Grand Rapids, MI 49525
Phone: 877-463-8379
www.verandadeck.com

WeatherBest
Louisiana-Pacific Corp.
414 Union St., Suite 2000
Nashville, TN 37219
www.weatherbest.com/

Tile

Daltile Corp.
7834 C.F. Hawn Frwy.
Dallas, TX 75217
Phone: 214-398-1411
www.daltileproducts.com

Wood

Southern Pine Council
P.O. Box 641700
Kenner, LA 70064
Phone: 504-443-4464
www.southernpine.com

Deck Fasteners

Climatek (coated screws)
GRK Fasteners
1499 Rosslyn Rd.
Thunder Bay, ON P7E 6W1
Canada
Phone: 800-263-0463
www.grkfasteners.com

Shadoe Track (fasteners)
Ty-Lan Enterprises, Inc.
London, ON
Canada
Phone: 800-742-3632
www.shadoetrack.com

Tiger Claw (hidden deck fasteners)
Tiger Claw, Inc.
400 Middle St., Suite J
Bristol, CT 06010
Phone: 800-928-4437
www.tigerclawinc.com

Floor-Leveling Compounds

Maxxon Corp.
920 Hamel Rd.
Hamel, MN 55340
Phone: 800-356-7887
www.maxxon.com

Finishes and Sealers

Olympic Paints and Stains
PPG Industries
One PPG Place
Pittsburgh, PA 15272
Phone: 412-434-3131
www.ppg.com/ppgaf/olympic

COLUMNS

These companies manufacture stock and custom columns and related items.

Chadsworth's 1.800.Columns
277 N. Front St.
Wilmington, NC 28401
Phone: 800-265-8667
www.columns.com

Colonial Columns
2102 Pasket Ln.
Houston, TX 77092
Phone: 877-681-2583
www.colonialcolumns.com

Melton Classics, Inc.
P.O. Box 465020
Lawrenceville, GA 30042
Phone: 800-963-3060
www.meltonclassics.com

Timeless Architectural Reproductions, Inc.
2655 Northgate Ave.
Cumming, GA 30041
Phone: 800-665-4341
www.timelessarchitectural.com

Internet Sources

These web sites provide listings of column manufacturers.

4specs.com
www.4specs.com/s/06/06404.html

USArchitecture.com
www.usarchitecture.com/Building_Supplies/columns.htm

ADDITIONAL RESOURCES

Computer-Aided Design

About.com
http://architecture.about.com/cs/cadprograms/tp/designsoftware.htm

SketchUp
@Last Software, Inc.
1433 Pearl St., Suite 100
Boulder, CO 80302
Phone: 303-245-0086
www.sketchup.com/

Outdoor Ceiling Fans

Casablanca Fan Co.
761 Corporate Center Dr.
Pomona, CA 91768
Phone: 888-227-2178
www.casablancafanco.com

Hunter Fan Co.
www.hunterfan.com

Stressed-Skin Panels (SIPs)

Porter Corp.
4240 N. 136th Ave.
Holland, MI 49424
Phone: 800-354-7721
www.portersips.com

Structural Insulated Panel Association
P.O. Box 1699
Gig Harbor, WA 98335
Phone: 253-858-7472
www.sips.org

Sun Angles

Use this web site to determine the angle of the sun at your latitude at any time of year.

U.S. Naval Observatory
http://aa.usno.navy.mil/data/docs/AltAz.html

GLOSSARY

Baluster One of the vertical supports for a handrail.

Batt insulation A mineral fiber material, delivered in rolls and typically paper- or foil-faced, that is installed between framing members to provide insulation.

Batten Narrow strips of wood that cover gaps between panels or boards on ceilings or walls.

Blind-nailing Placement of nails in tongue-and-groove boards so the nails are covered by the joint.

Building code Design and material specifications governing construction in a given municipality or geographical area.

Cast stone A mixture of materials poured into a mold or form to create architectural elements that appear to be made of stone.

Caulk Flexible materials used to fill seams and gaps to prevent air or water penetration.

Cement board Cement-based backer board used as an underlayment for ceramic tile.

Clapboard A narrow board, tapered in cross section, applied in lapped courses for house siding.

Column A vertical support member, typically with a cylindrical or square shaft. Also called a pillar. Classical column designs include a base, shaft, and capital.

Cornice Any molding (typically large) or group of moldings surmounting a wall or at the junction of a wall and ceiling.

Crawl space An accessible area between the ground and decking or floor of a porch or other structure.

Divided lights A window formed by panes of glass set into a gridlike framework.

Double-hung window A window comprising an upper and lower sash, each of which can move vertically past the other.

Drywall Gypsum sandwiched between treated paper. Used as an interior covering material. Also called gypsum board or wallboard.

Eaves The part of a roof that projects beyond its supporting walls to create an overhang.

Facade The visible exterior of a building.

Face-nailing Placement of nails so that the heads are visible on the surface of a board; the heads are often driven beneath the surface and covered with putty.

Fascia Trim pieces covering the ends of rafters at the base of a roof.

Fiberglass Spun-glass fibers used in insulation and roof shingles.

Flashing Thin strips of metal used to form a weatherproof seal where a roof meets a wall, in a roof valley, or at a horizontal junction of a window or door and any part of a structure.

Flat sawing The technique of milling boards parallel to a diameter of a tree trunk.

Footing The base, usually poured concrete, supporting a foundation wall or posts, columns, or piers.

Foundation Substructure, usually below ground and made of concrete or masonry, supporting a porch or other structure.

Framing The structural skeleton, typically wood, of a house.

Gable roof A triangular shaped roof.

Galvanized metal Coated with zinc to prevent rusting.

Hardwood Generally, the wood of large deciduous trees such as maple, oak, and poplar.

Header Horizontal supporting member, such as a beam or lintel, spanning the top of a wall opening. Also the decorative trim assembly over an opening.

Hip roof A roof that has a central ridge and that slopes in at least three directions.

Insulated glass Usually sealed double-pane glass units with a vacuum or gas in the space between the panes.

Joists Horizontal framing members of a floor or ceiling frame.

Lag screw A large screw with a pointed tip and a hex head.

Ledger A horizontal board firmly attached to a wall or frame to support joists or rafters of a porch or other addition.

Load bearing Refering to a wall or other support that helps carry significant structural weight.

Low-E Low-emissivity coating. A microscopically thin metal or metal oxide film applied to the inside surfaces of double-pane glass to reduce heat gain.

Masking Covering a surface when painting near it, usually with masking tape.

Masonry wall A wall made of concrete block, brick, stone, or sometimes poured concrete.

Molding Decorative strips of wood or other materials used in various kinds of trimwork.

Oriented strand board (OSB) A panel made of wood strands purposely aligned for strength and bonded by phenolic resin.

Overhang The part of the tail end of a rafter that projects beyond the building line. Often it is enclosed by a soffit.

Pedestal A base of a column, sculpture, or architectural ornament.

Pier A masonry support equivalent to a wooden post.

Pilaster A shallow, square-edged column projecting from a wall or other vertical surface. Typically, a decorative treatment made to appear as a supporting element.

Pitch Loosely, the slope or angle of a roof; technically, the rise of a roof over its span.

Plinth A distinct structural element serving as the base of a wall, column, pedestal, or pilaster.

Plumb An expression describing a perfectly vertical surface or line. A plumb surface will meet a level surface at 90 degrees to form a right angle.

Plywood A panel composed of cross-laminated wood veneers.

Post A shaft, usually made of wood or metal, that provides support at a specific point on a structure.

Post-and-beam framing A construction method employing widely spaced stout horizontal (post) and vertical (beam) members in the main structure.

Precast concrete Building elements (such as entry steps) made of reinforced concrete in a factory.

Pressure treatment A factory process of using pressure to force preservatives into wood.

Quartersawing The technique of milling boards so that their faces coincide approximately with radii from the center of the tree trunk; typically very stable close-grained wood.

Rafters The principal supporting members of a roof frame, spanning between the walls and the roof peak or ridge.

Ridgeboard The horizontal board that defines the roof's highest point or ridge.

Ridge cap Shingles or other covering spanning a roof ridge.

Ridge vent A nearly continuous opening, shielded from weather, along a roof ridge to permit ventilation of the roof structure.

R-value "R" is the measure of a substance's resistance to heat flow. An "R" value is a number assigned to insulation. The higher the number, the better the insulation.

Setback The distance required by code or regulation between a structure and a street, sidewalk, or property line.

Sheathing Panels or boards applied to a building's framework beneath siding or roofing.

Shed roof A roof that slopes in one direction only.

Slab floor A concrete surface poured at ground level or on an above-ground framework to serve as a floor.

Soffit The material used to cover the underside of roof eaves.

Softwood Generally, the wood of coniferous, needle-bearing trees such as pine, fir, or spruce.

Stave-built A form, usually curved, made of a series of narrow boards joined edge to edge.

Stressed-skin panel A structural unit comprising a rigid foam core glued to two outer skins made of plywood, OSB, or metal.

Structural column A load-bearing architectural column that may also be decorative.

Stucco Cement-based, waterproof exterior wall covering applied like plaster.

Studs The vertical members of a wall frame.

Subfloor Panels or boards installed on joists as a base for finished flooring.

Substrate Material, often a panel or concrete slab, that supports a surface material, such as veneer or ceramic tile.

Thermal break A separation, filled with a non-heat-conductive material, between components of a metal structural member to lessen the transfer of heat from one component to the other.

Tongue and groove Features milled onto opposite edges of a board so that similar boards can fit together to form a self-aligning, interlocking surface.

Underlayment Highly stable, often water-resistant panels installed on top of a subfloor to support resilient flooring or other finish flooring material.

U-value A measure of a material's facilitation of heat transfer. The lower the value, the less heat conducted.

Vapor barrier A thin membrane, usually plastic, applied to a wall or other surface to prevent the migration of water vapor.

Vertical grain A term often used for flooring or stair treads to indicate that the growth rings are perpendicular to the faces of the boards, making the boards more resistant to wear.

Vinyl glazing A flexible but tough plastic used in windows instead of glass.

PHOTO & DESIGNER CREDITS

page 1: Rick Mastelli **page 2:** Roger Bruhn **page 6:** *top* Rick Mastelli; *bottom* Rick Mastelli, architect: Truex Cullins and Partners, builder: Bradley Construction **page 7:** courtesy of Renaissance Conservatories **page 8:** Jessie Walker Associates **page 10:** *top* Rick Mastelli; *bottom* courtesy of Hostetler Patio Enclosures, Inc. **page 11:** Donna Chiarelli Photography **page 12:** courtesy of Renaissance Conservatories **page 13:** *top* Rick Mastelli; *bottom* Donna Chiarelli Photography **page 16:** *top* Donna Chiarelli Photography; *bottom* Jessie Walker Associates, designer: Adele Lampert **page 17:** *top* Roger Holmes; *bottom* courtesy of Maureen Allman **page 18:** *top* courtesy of SketchUp, *bottom* Roger Bruhn **page 19:** Jessie Walker Associates **page 21:** Jessie Walker Associates **page 22:** *both* Jessie Walker Associates; *bottom* designer: Barbara Metzler **page 24:** Jessie Walker Associates **page 25:** Donna Chiarelli Photography **pages 26–29:** *all* Jessie Walker Associates **page 30:** Jessie Walker Associates, designer: Greene & Proppe Designs **page 31:** Jessie Walker Associates **page 32:** *both* Jessie Walker Associates, architect: Stephen Knutson **page 34:** Jessie Walker Associates **page 35:** *both* courtesy of Hostetler Patio Enclosures, Inc. **page 36:** *top* Rick Mastelli; *bottom* Jessie Walker Associates **page 37:** Jessie Walker Associates **page 38:** *both* Jessie Walker Associates **page 39:** Jessie Walker Associates, designer: Barbara Metzler **page 40:** Jessie Walker Associates, architect: George Pappageorge **page 41:** *both* Jessie Walker Associates; *bottom* architect: David Ogden **page 42:** Donna Chiarelli Photography, designer: Joanne Kostecky Garden Design **page 44:** Jessie Walker Associates **page 45:** Roger Holmes **page 46:** *both* courtesy of Hostetler Patio Enclosures, Inc. **page 47:** Rick Mastelli **page 48:** Jessie Walker Associates **page 49:** Jessie Walker Associates **page 50:** courtesy of Hostetler Patio Enclosures, Inc. **page 51:** *both* courtesy of Hostetler Patio Enclosures, Inc. **page 52:** Jessie Walker Associates **page 53:** Jessie Walker Associates **page 54:** *top* Roger Holmes; *bottom* Stephen Pategas, HortusOasis **page 55:** *top* courtesy of Patricia Lombardi; *bottom* Roger Bruhn **page 56:** *both* courtesy of Hostetler Patio Enclosures, Inc. **page 57:** *all* Donna Chiarelli Photography, designer: Custom Patio Sunrooms **page 58:** *left* Roger Bruhn; *right* Donna Chiarelli Photography **page 59:** Jessie Walker Associates **page 60:** *both* courtesy of Hostetler Patio Enclosures, Inc. **page 61:** *both* Donna Chiarelli Photography **page 62:** *both* courtesy of Hostetler Patio Enclosures, Inc. **page 63:** *top* Donna Chiarelli Photography, designer: Joanne Kostecky Garden Design; *bottom* Jessie Walker Associates **page 64:** Jessie Walker Associates **page 66:** Jessie Walker Associates, designer: Adele Lampert/Interiors II **page 67:** *top* Jessie Walker Associates; *bottom* Donna Chiarelli Photography **page 68:** *both* Rick Mastelli **page 69:** Rick Mastelli, architect: Truex Cullins and Partners, builder: Bradley Construction **page 70:** *all* Roger Bruhn **page 71:** Rick Mastelli **page 73:** Jessie Walker Associates **page 74:** Roger Bruhn **page 76:** *top* courtesy of Armstrong Urban Challenge; *bottom* Jessie Walker Associates **page 77:** Jessie Walker Associates **page 78:** Rick Mastelli **page 79:** *top left* courtesy of EverGrain; *top right* Rick Mastelli; *bottom* Jessie Walker Associates **page 80:** *right* Roger Holmes; *left* Donna Chiarelli Photography **page 81:** *top right* Roger Bruhn; *bottom left* Roger Holmes; *bottom right* Roger Holmes **page 82:** Rick Mastelli **page 83:** Donna Chiarelli Photography **page 84:** *both* Donna Chiarelli Photography **page 85:** Rick Mastelli, architect: Truex Cullins and Partners, builder: Bradley Construction **page 86:** *all* Roger Holmes **page 88:** *top left* Rick Mastelli; *top right* Roger Bruhn; *bottom* Jessie Walker Associates **page 89:** Roger Holmes **page 90:** *left* Roger Bruhn; *right* Donna Chiarelli Photography **page 92:** *top and bottom left* Donna Chiarelli Photography; *bottom right* Rick Mastelli **page 93:** *both* Rick Mastelli **page 94:** *top* Donna Chiarelli Photography; *bottom* Jessie Walker Associates **page 95:** Rick Mastelli **page 96:** Roger Holmes **page 97:** *left and top right* Rick Mastelli; *bottom right* Roger Holmes **page 98:** Rick Mastelli **page 99:** *top and center left* Roger Bruhn; *bottom left* Roger Holmes; *right* Rick Mastelli **page 100:** *left and top right* Roger Holmes; *bottom right* Roger Bruhn **page 101:** Jessie Walker Associates **page 102:** Donna Chiarelli Photography **page 103:** courtesy of Hostetler Patio Enclosures, Inc. **page 104:** *top* Roger Holmes; *bottom* Roger Bruhn **page 105:** *top* Jessie Walker Associates; *bottom* Rick Mastelli **page 106:** *left* Rick Mastelli, architect: Truex Cullins and Partners, builder: Bradley Construction; *right* Donna Chiarelli Photography **page 107:** *both* Donna Chiarelli Photography **page 108:** *both* Rick Mastelli **page 109:** *top left* Roger Holmes; *top right* courtesy of Gregg and Emily Lanik; *bottom right* Roger Bruhn **page 110:** *both* Jessie Walker Associates, designer: Gavin Mullin **page 111:** *both* Jessie Walker Associates **page 112:** *both* Jessie Walker Associates **page 113:** *top* Jessie Walker Associates; *bottom* courtesy of Armstrong Urban Challenge **page 114:** *left* Rick Mastelli; *right* Roger Holmes **page 115:** Jessie Walker Associates **page 116:** Jessie Walker Associates **page 118:** *both* courtesy of Hostetler Patio Enclosures, Inc. **page 121:** *left* Roger Bruhn; *top and bottom right* courtesy of Hostetler Patio Enclosures, Inc. **page 122:** *top left* Jessie Walker Associates; *top right* Jessie Walker Associates, designer: Adele Lampert/Interiors II; *bottom* Roger Holmes **page 123:** Jessie Walker Associates **page 124:** Jessie Walker Associates **page 125:** *all* courtesy of Hostetler Patio Enclosures, Inc. **page 126** *both* courtesy of Hostetler Patio Enclosures, Inc. **page 127:** Jessie Walker Associates **page 128:** Jessie Walker Associates, builder: Nelson Log Homes **page 129:** *all* courtesy of Hostetler Patio Enclosures, Inc. **page 130–131:** *all* Donna Chiarelli Photography, designer: Custom Patio Sunrooms **page 133:** Jessie Walker Associates **page 135:** Jessie Walker Associates **page 136:** courtesy of Crossville, Inc. **page 137:** Jessie Walker Associates, design: Suzanne Murphy Designs **page 138:** Jessie Walker Associates **page 139:** Jessie Walker Associates **page 140:** Jessie Walker Associates, design: Lorrie Browne, stylist: Pilar Simone **page 141:** Roger Holmes **page 142:** *both* Jessie Walker Associates; *bottom* designer: Ryan Carter/Brit Carter Furniture **page 143:** Jessie Walker Associates, designer: Meredith Moriarty **page 144:** courtesy of Hostetler Patio Enclosures, Inc. **page 145:** *top* Jessie Walker Associates; *bottom* courtesy of Daltile **page 146:** *both* Jessie Walker Associates; *top* designers: Elizabeth Burden Cassier & Gayle Dahling Veach; *bottom* designer: Marilynn Davis **page 149:** *top* courtesy of National Fenestration Ratings Council, Inc.; *bottom* courtesy of ENERGY STAR **page 150:** *both* Jessie Walker Associates **page 151:** Jessie Walker Associates, designer: Dave McFadden **page 152:** *all* Rick Mastelli **page 153:** Donna Chiarelli Photography, designer: Custom Patio Sunrooms **page 154:** courtesy of Crossville, Inc. **page 155:** courtesy of Hostetler Patio Enclosures, Inc. **page 156:** Jessie Walker Associates, architect: Stephan Knutson **page 157:** courtesy of Hostetler Patio Enclosures, Inc. **page 159:** *all* courtesy of Hostetler Patio Enclosures, Inc. **page 161:** Jessie Walker Associates, designer: Linda Brown **page 162:** courtesy of Hostetler Patio Enclosures, Inc. **page 163:** Donna Chiarelli Photography, designer: Custom Patio Sunrooms **page 164:** Jessie Walker Associates **page 165:** Jessie Walker Associates, designer: Diane Wendell **page 166:** Jessie Walker Associates **page 168:** *top* courtesy of Renaissance Conservatories; *bottom* courtesy of Colebrook Conservatories **page 169:** *top* courtesy of Renaissance Conservatories; *bottom* Rick Mastelli **page 170:** courtesy of Hostetler Patio Enclosures, Inc. **page 171:** courtesy of Renaissance Conservatories **page 172:** *top* courtesy of Renaissance Conservatories; *bottom* courtesy of Hostetler Patio Enclosures, Inc. **page 173:** courtesy of Renaissance Conservatories **page 174:** *left* courtesy of Colebrook Conservatories; *right* Rick Mastelli, architect: Lawrence Atkin, manufacturer: Amdega **page 175:** *bottom* Jessie Walker Associates **page 176:** Roger Bruhn **page 177:** *left* Roger Bruhn; *top and bottom right* Rick Mastelli **page 178:** courtesy of Renaissance Conservatories **page 179:** courtesy of Hostetler Patio Enclosures, Inc. **page 180:** Rick Mastelli, Architect: Lawrence Atkin, Manufacturer: Amdega **page 181:** courtesy of Renaissance Conservatories **page 182:** *both* courtesy of Renaissance Conservatories **page 183:** *right* courtesy of Colebrook Conservatories **page 185:** courtesy of Renaissance Conservatories **page 187:** *top* Roger Bruhn; *bottom* Jessie Walker Associates **page 188:** *both* Rick Mastelli, Architect: Lawrence Atkin, Manufacturer: Amdega **page 189:** Jessie Walker Associates **page 190:** Roger Bruhn **page 192** *top* Roger Bruhn; *bottom* Rick Mastelli **page 193:** Donna Chiarelli Photography **page 194:** Roger Holmes **page 196:** *all* Roger Bruhn **page 197:** Roger Bruhn **page 198:** Rick Mastelli **page 199:** Roger Bruhn **page 200:** *top* Rick Mastelli; *bottom* Roger Bruhn **pages 201–206:** *all* Roger Bruhn **page 207:** *top left and right* Roger Holmes; *bottom left* Roger Bruhn **page 208:** *top* Rick Mastelli; *bottom* Roger Bruhn **page 209:** Rick Mastelli **page 210:** Rick Mastelli **page 211** courtesy of Crossville, Inc. **page 212:** Donna Chiarelli Photography **page 215:** Jesse Walker Associates **page 219:** Rick Mastelli

Photographers

Jessie Walker Associates
Glencoe, IL
847-835-0522
www.jessiewalker.com

Donna Chiarelli Photography
Kutztown, PA
610-683-7574
www.dhcstudio.com

Roger Bruhn Photography
Lincoln, NE
402-474-6434

Rick Mastelli
Image & Word
Montpelier, VT
802-229-1320

INDEX

Bold page numbers refer to illustrations and sidebars.

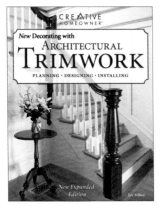

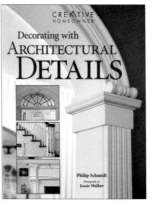

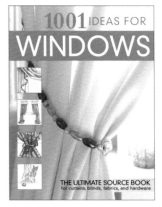

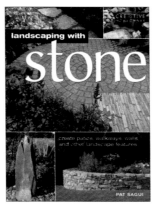

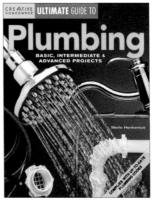

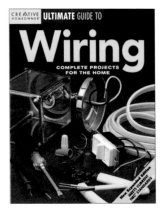

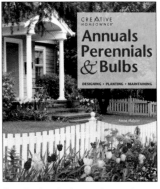

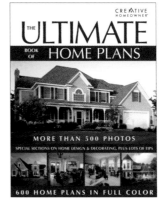

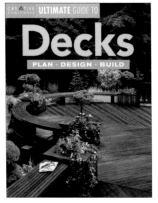

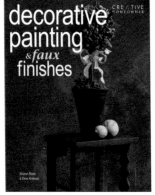

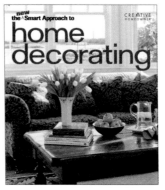

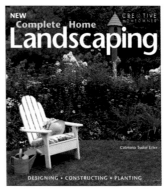